Integrated Algebra on the TI-73

Kathleen Noftsier

TRAFFORD
PUBLISHING

Order this book online at www.trafford.com
or email orders@trafford.com

Most Trafford titles are also available at major online book retailers.

Printed in the United States of America.

ISBN: 978-1-4269-4329-4 (sc)
ISBN: 978-1-4269-4328-7 (e)

Trafford rev. 01/13/2011

www.trafford.com

North America & international
toll-free: 1 888 232 4444 (USA & Canada)
phone: 250 383 6864 ♦ fax: 812 355 4082

Table of Contents

Graphing Calculator for NYS Integrated Algebra

This graphing calculator workbook is designed to:

1. Give you alternate strategies for solving math problems you have already learned how to solve or calculate in your Integrated Algebra class.

2. Give extra practice on regents-type questions.

3. Demonstrate how to work around "quirks" in the programming of the calculator.

4. Begin developing skills needed for the Geometry and Algebra 2/Trigonometry exams, and college calculus and statistics courses.

**Note that some topics go beyond the scope of the Integrated Algebra exam. This is to help justify giving math credit for those schools that choose to use this as a text for a mathematics elective. They can be omitted if the workbook is used as a supplement to a course leading to the Integrated Algebra regents.

The exercises in this book were designed to be completed with the TI-73 graphing calculator. Many can also be completed with the TI-83+/TI-84+ graphing calculator.

Beware!! These calculators are designed to work with TI applications only. Do not download non-TI applications or programs to your calculator. It can cause your calculator to work inefficiently or disable your operating system! Some can work in the same way a virus affects your PC!

Protect your calculator! Whether you have your own, or are responsible for a school-owned calculator, you should know how to identify the calculator.
There are two identification numbers.
  1. The first is on the outside. Find the number on the back of the calculator you will be responsible for (yours or the school's) and record it here: _____
  2. The second is an internal number. To find it:
      a. Turn the calculator on.
      b. Go to Memory (2nd, 0).
      c. Choose 1:About
      d. Look for ID:
      e. Write the calculator's ID# here: _____
      f. Your signature: _____

You should also note the number under the product name. This is the number of the current operating system (OS). The operating system should be updated so that the most current system is loaded to ensure the best performance.

At this time, the most current OS for the TI 73 is: _____

If your calculator has an OS lower than this it should be updated at the earliest opportunity.

A note about the pages marked

Regents Connection

These are collections of Algebra regents questions on the topic immediately preceding the section. They are not all intended to be done on the graphing calculator. They are meant as an opportunity to practice questions for the regents exam. They should also provide an opportunity to discern which questions can be done on the calculator for the Algebra exam and which should be completed using other methods.

Good luck and happy calculating!

Knowing Your Calculator

Let's start at the top. The graphing calculator screen is made up of

_____ .

There are _____ across and _____ down.

This limits the way that numbers, letters, and graphs appear on our screen.

Pixels are _____

_____ .

Although they are technically NOT little squares, on the calculator screen we can think of them that way.   On the next page is a grid made of the same number of "pixels' as your calculator screen.

Take a few minutes to create a picture by filling in squares on the grid.

It should be apparent why we cannot make smooth looking lines or curves. This will be especially important when we begin to graph and we cannot "see" exactly how the lines or curves are connected as we move from pixel to pixel.

Graphs may also not be _____ correctly because the number of pixels in each direction is different.

The screen can hold _____ lines with _____ characters per line. If your entry has more characters the calculator will "wrap" to the next line.

Your entries will appear from left to right. The answer will appear on the right when you press ENTER .

When you exceed 8 lines the lines at the top of the screen will disappear. You can go back to these using the _____ _____ .

Try a few simple calculations. Continue until your first calculation has disappeared from the screen.

Use the up arrow to scroll back up through your calculations. With an expression highlighted (as opposed to an answer) press ENTER . What happens?

_____

_____

(This may be handy later when you want to reenter a calculation!)

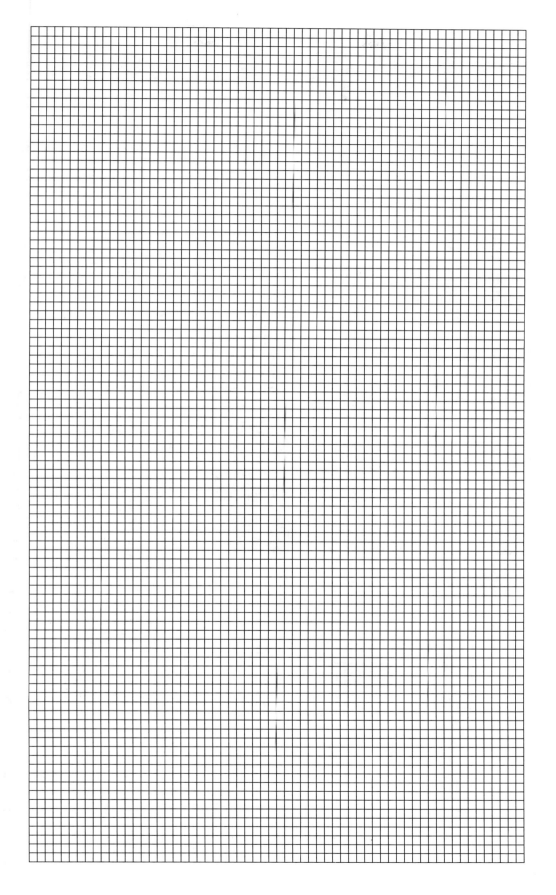

Below the screen are the SOFT KEYS.

| Y= | WINDOW | ZOOM | TRACE | GRAPH |

Applications often make use of these keys. They are also your basic tools for graphing. We will look at these closer later.

On the next row of keys, the first key is the 2ND key. It allows us to use the functions on any main key that is written in yellow above the key. List the "2nd" function for each of the keys below:

MODE _____

DEL _____

MATH _____

DRAW _____

LIST _____

X² _____

^ _____

PRGM _____

APPS _____

ENTER _____

UNIT _____

b/c _____

F ↔ D _____

CONST _____

÷ _____

STO → _____

ON _____

0 _____

(−) _____

Many of these features we will wait to learn about when we need them, but there are a few that are especially important and useful in our general use of the calculator. Let's look at these now.

	[2ND] [ON]	Turns the calculator off, although the calculator will turn off by itself in about 5 minutes.
	[2ND] [▲]	Darkens the screen (be sure to hold down the arrow until it as dark as you need it).
	[2ND] [▼]	Lightens the screen
	[2ND] [PRGM]	***The catalog contains all of the functions and symbols available on the calculator!
	[2ND] [MODE]	This will take you back to the home screen from wherever else you might be.
	[2ND] [DEL]	Move the cursor to where you want to insert a symbol or function.
	[2ND] [MATH]	The alphabet and some symbols are available from this menu.
	[2ND] [(−)]	This will allow you to use the ANSWER from the previous calculation anywhere in your current calculation.
	[2ND] [ENTER]	This command is like a "backspace" key to go back to previous calculations. You can recalculate the same calculation or edit it if you want to make a small change or correction in a complex calculation.

You may have noticed by now that the keys are color-coded:

The _____ ,

_____ , and _____

_____ are white.

The _____ _____ ,

_____ and _____ _____ are red.

The keys used for _____ have a blue base but a white face and blue print.

The _____ _____ , as we noted before, is bright yellow.

The remaining keys are blue with white print. We will take a closer look at these as we need them.

At the base of the calculator you should notice a small hole. With a unit-to-unit linking cable you can connect to another calculator to send lists, programs, or applications. With a computer cable you can connect to a computer and transfer files that have been saved from a calculator or downloaded from the TI website. You can also update your operating system by linking with another calculator or computer.

See the appendix for more details on how to link and receive/send.

The Basics

Unless you plan to always have two calculators handy, it is best to first make sure we can use the graphing calculator to do all of our basic calculating!

The operation keys are along the right side of the calculator:

The TI-73 is a handheld computer, so when you want to finish an operation you press

_____

(Like a computer!)

Notation: When you press the [X] key you know that this means

_____ or finding the _____

On the calculator it will appear as an asterisk (*).

The calculator will also recognize parentheses as multiplication. For example, 5×29 , $5 * 29$, and $(5)(29)$ mean the same thing to the calculator.

Also, when you press [÷] the calculator screen will not show "÷" , it will display

the division with this symbol: "/"

To square a number or expression, press [X²]

To raise a number to any other power use this key: [^]

Some references will call this a "carat" key, others will call it the "power" key. They are both correct and mean the same thing.

Then you can evaluate (_____) 3^3 by pressing

[3] [^] [3]

What is 3^3 ?   _____

This method will work for any power. (Including squaring.) There is an alternative for

finding a cube of a number. With the number on the homescreen, press [MATH]

and choose 3:³ then press [ENTER]

This calculator will also do division the "old fashioned" way. Remember long division and finding remainders? The TI-73 will find an answer in this form.
Try this:

Divide 39 by 2 by pressing

 3   9   2ND   ÷   2   ENTER

What is the result? _____

This says that _____

_____

Practice:

1. Evaluate: $345 - 238 + 146$ _____

2. Evaluate: 459×34 _____

3. Evaluate: $56.82 \div 3$ _____

4. Evaluate: $45 + 29 - 57 * 4 + 38 \div 2$ _____

5. Evaluate: $\sqrt{144}$ _____

6. Evaluate: $5 + \sqrt{169}$ _____

7. Evaluate: $7 \div \sqrt{400}$ _____

8. Evaluate: 7^3 _____

9. Evaluate: 15^5 _____

10. Find the **remainder**: $58 \div 8$ _____

11. Find the remainder: $1057 \div 13$ _____

12. Find the remainder: $3456 \div 4$ _____

Order of Operations

To use the calculator effectively we need to understand the order of operations.

Although the calculator has its own order of operations called its _____ , this system is based on our familiar order of operations:

P _____

E _____

M&D _____

_____

A&S _____

_____

EOS™ stands for _____ _____ _____

and is trademarked by Texas Instruments.

The EOS™ for the TI-73 is:

1. _____

2. _____

3. _____

4. _____

5. _____

6. _____

7. _____

8. _____

9. _____

10. _____

How does the EOS™ compare with our familiar PEMDAS? Describe the similarities and/or differences.

_____

_____

_____

_____

_____

**Like PEMDAS the EOS will also work from left to right with operations that are on the same "level".

Why is this important to understand?

Most of the operations will work fine if we enter them the way they appear on paper, but there is one important difference. Fill in the chart below entering the expressions exactly as they appear.

$2^2 =$	$-2^2 =$	$(-2)^2 =$
$2^3 =$	$-2^3 =$	$(-2)^3 =$
$2^4 =$	$-2^4 =$	$(-2)^4 =$
$2^5 =$	$-2^5 =$	$(-2)^5 =$
$2^6 =$	$-2^6 =$	$(-2)^6 =$

Is there a pattern for when the last column matches the first and when it matches the second column? Explain.

_____

_____

_____

This occurs because the calculator reads negative numbers in a way we don't normally think of them. When you enter a negative number in the calculator you see your negative number, but the calculator sees _____ _____

_____

_____ .

So when you entered -2^2 in the calculator it really read it as _____ ,
Which operation will the calculator perform first? _____ .
Then it will _____ . This results in a negative answer when we know it should be positive. How should you work with negative numbers raised to powers?
Two methods are reliable:

1. Always use parenthesis.

    OR

2. Store your number to x, then raise x to the power. See the screen shots on the next page.

Example:

Let's find -5^2 both ways.

1. Using the square or the power key:

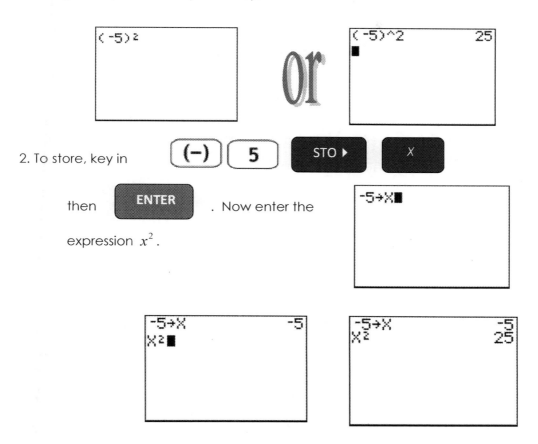

2. To store, key in (−) 5 STO ► X

   then ENTER . Now enter the

   expression x^2.

Practice: Simplify the following expressions.

1. -3^4 _____

2. -5^3 _____

3. -6^2 _____

4. -1^{20} _____

5. -8^4 _____

6. -10^{-2} *****Always place negative or fraction exponents in parentheses also!!!

_____

7. How does the calculator read the expression -4^6 ? _____

**8. How does the calculator read the expression 2^{-4} ? _____

On a related note, we should explore how the calculator deals with parentheses. Enter each of the following expressions in the calculator exactly as they appear:

$$\sqrt{4}+3 = \underline{\hspace{2cm}} \qquad\qquad \sqrt{(4)}+3 = \underline{\hspace{2cm}}$$

You should have noticed that the calculator automatically inserts parentheses immediately after the square root symbol. The square root symbol can't be extended so we must use some other way to tell the calculator what should be under the radical Because we didn't end the parentheses in the first expression the calculator thinks we meant $\sqrt{4+3}$. Unfortunately, the calculator thinks we are lazy – it allows us to leave off a closing parentheses with no error message. This will cause incorrect results if we are not careful!! Bottom line – always end your parentheses!! (Even when the calculator starts them for you.)

Practice:

Simplify the following expressions.

1. $\sqrt{25}+7$ \underline{\hspace{3cm}}

2. $\sqrt{100}-\sqrt{4}$ \underline{\hspace{3cm}}

3. $\sqrt{9+7}-\sqrt{121}$ \underline{\hspace{3cm}}

4. $\sqrt{49}+\sqrt{169}$ \underline{\hspace{3cm}}

5. $3-\sqrt{4+21}-\sqrt{64}+81$ \underline{\hspace{3cm}}

6. $5+\sqrt{400}-\sqrt{144}$ \underline{\hspace{3cm}}

7. $\sqrt{49}-3^2$ \underline{\hspace{3cm}}

8. $-5^2-\sqrt{36}$ \underline{\hspace{3cm}}

9. $\sqrt{-4^2-7}$ \underline{\hspace{3cm}}

10. $\sqrt{-4^2}-7$ \underline{\hspace{3cm}}

Regents Connection

Basic Operations

<u>June '99, #11:</u> The expression $2^3 \bullet 4^2$ is equivalent to

    (1) 2^7 (2) 2^{12} (3) 8^5 (4) 8^6

_____

<u>June '99, #20:</u> The expression $\sqrt{27} + \sqrt{12}$ is equivalent to

    (1) $5\sqrt{3}$ (2) $13\sqrt{3}$ (3) $5\sqrt{6}$ (4) $\sqrt{39}$

_____

<u>Jan '00, #1:</u> The expression $\sqrt{93}$ is a number between

    (1) 3 and 9   (3) 9 and 10
    (2) 8 and 9   (4) 46 and 47

_____

<u>Jan '00, #2:</u> Which number has the greatest value?

    (1) $1\frac{2}{3}$ (2) $\sqrt{2}$ (3) $\frac{\pi}{2}$ (4) 1.5

_____

<u>Aug '99, #2:</u> the expression $\sqrt{50}$ can be simplified to

    (1) $5\sqrt{2}$ (2) $5\sqrt{10}$ (3) $2\sqrt{25}$ (4) $25\sqrt{2}$

_____

<u>Aug '99, #14:</u> In a hockey league, 87 players play on seven different teams. Each team has at least 12 players. What is the largest possible number of players on any one team?

    (1) 13   (2) 14   (3) 15   (4) 21

_____

<u>June '00, #20:</u> What is the value of 3^{-2}?

    (1) $\dfrac{1}{9}$ (2) $-\dfrac{1}{9}$ (3) 9   (4) -9

_____

<u>Sample #19:</u> The expression $\sqrt{150}$ is equivalent to

    (1) $25\sqrt{6}$ (2) $15\sqrt{10}$ (3) $5\sqrt{6}$ (4) $6\sqrt{5}$

_____

<u>Jan '03, #11:</u> The sum of $\sqrt{75}$ and $\sqrt{3}$ is

    (1) 15   (2) 18   (3) $6\sqrt{3}$ (4) $\sqrt{78}$

_____

<u>June '03, #12:</u> The expression $3^2 \bullet 3^3 \bullet 3^4$ is equivalent to

    (1) 27^9 (2) 27^{24} (3) 3^9 (4) 3^{24}

_____

<u>June '03, #16:</u> The sum of $\sqrt{18}$ and $\sqrt{72}$ is

    (1) $\sqrt{90}$ (2) $9\sqrt{2}$ (3) $3\sqrt{10}$ (4) $6\sqrt{3}$

_____

<u>Jan '04, #3:</u> On February 18, from 9 a.m. until 2 p.m., the temperature rose from $-14°F$ to $36°F$. What was the total increase in temperature during this time period?

    (1) $50°$ (2) $36°$ (3) $32°$ (4) $22°$

_____

<u>Jan '04, #13:</u> The expression $8^{-4} \bullet 8^6$ is equivalent to

    (1) 8^{-24} (2) 8^{-2} (3) 8^2 (4) 8^{10}

_____

June '04, #33: Kyoko's mathematics teacher gave her the accompanying cards and asked her to arrange the cards in order from least to greatest. In what order should Kyoko arrange the cards?

_____   _____   _____   _____   _____

Jan '10, #20: Which expression is equivalent to $3^3 \bullet 3^4$?

    (1) 9^{12} (2) 9^7 (3) 3^{12} (4) 3^7

                                                            _____

Jun '08, #13: What is half of 2^6 ?

    (1) 1^3 (2) 1^6 (3) 2^3 (4) 2^5

                                                              _____

Regents Connection

Properties of Real Numbers

June '99, #23: Which number below is irrational?

$$\sqrt{\frac{4}{9}}, \ \sqrt{20}, \ \sqrt{121}$$

Why is the number you chose an irrational number?

_____

_____

_____

Jan '00, #6: If the number represented by $n-3$ is an odd integer, which expression represents the next greater odd integer?

    (1) $n-5$ (2) $n-2$ (3) $n-1$ (4) $n+1$

_____

June '01, #8: Which equation illustrates the distributive property for real numbers?

    (1) $\dfrac{1}{3}+\dfrac{1}{2}=\dfrac{1}{2}+\dfrac{1}{3}$

    (2) $\sqrt{3}+0=\sqrt{3}$

    (3) $(1.3 \bullet 0.07) \bullet 0.63 = 1.3 \bullet (0.07 \bullet 0.63)$

    (4) $-3(5+7)=(-3)(5)+(-3)(7)$

_____

June '01, #13: If a is an odd number, b an even number, and c an odd number, which expression will always be equivalent to an odd number?

    (1) $a(bc)$ (3) $ac(b)^{1}$

    (2) $ac(b)^{0}$ (4) $ac(b)^{2}$

_____

June '01, #20: Which is a rational number?

    (1) $\sqrt{8}$ (2) π (3) $5\sqrt{9}$ (4) $6\sqrt{2}$

_____

<u>Aug '99, #7:</u> Which equation is an illustration of the additive identity property?

(1) $x \bullet 1 = x$

(3) $x - x = 0$

(2) $x + 0 = x$

(4) $x \bullet \dfrac{1}{x} = 1$

_____

<u>Aug '99, #28:</u> Bob and Ray are describing the same number. Bob says, "The number is a positive integer less than or equal to 20." Ray says, "The number is divisible by 4." If Bob's statement is true and Ray's statement is false, what are all the possible numbers?

_____

<u>Jan '01, #3:</u> If $x > 0$, the expression $(\sqrt{x})(\sqrt{2x})$ is equivalent to

(1) $\sqrt{2x}$

(2) $2x$

(3) $x^2\sqrt{2}$

(4) $x\sqrt{2}$

_____

<u>Jan '01, #7:</u> If a and b are integers, which equation is always true?

(1) $\dfrac{a}{b} = \dfrac{b}{a}$

(3) $a - b = b - a$

(2) $a + 2b = b + 2a$

(4) $a + b = b + a$

_____

<u>Aug '00, #6:</u> If $a < b$, $c < d$, and a, b, c, and d are all greater than 0, which expression is always true?

(1) $a - c + b - d$

(3) $\dfrac{a}{d} > \dfrac{b}{c}$

(2) $a + c > b + d$

(4) $ac < bd$

_____

<u>Jan '02, #17:</u> Which set is closed under division?

(1) {1}

(3) integers

(2) counting numbers

(4) whole numbers

_____

<u>Aug '02, #8:</u> The number $0.14114111411114\ldots$ is

(1) integral

(2) rational

(3) irrational

(4) whole

_____

<u>Jan '01, #20</u>: Let x and y be numbers such that $0 < x < y < 1$, and let $d = x - y$. Which graph could represent the location of d on the number line?

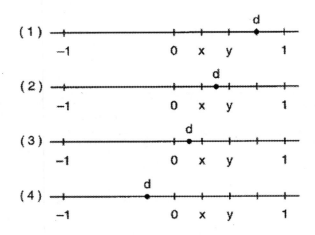

<u>Aug '00, #10</u>: The operation $*$ for the set $\{p, r, s, v\}$ is defined in the accompanying table. What is the inverse element of r under the operation $*$?

$*$	p	r	s	v
p	s	v	p	r
r	v	p	r	s
s	p	r	s	v
v	r	s	v	p

(1) p (2) r (3) s (4) v

<u>Aug '01, #2</u>: Which expression is rational?

(1) π (2) $\sqrt{\dfrac{1}{2}}$ (3) $\sqrt{3}$ (4) $\sqrt{\dfrac{1}{4}}$

<u>Jan '02, #21</u>: Seth is thinking of a number between 20 and 30. The number is prime and not more than 2 away from a perfect square. What is the number?

<u>Aug '01, #12:</u> The operation element @ is determined by the following table:

@	a	b	c
a	a	b	c
b	b	c	a
c	c	a	b

What is the identity element of this operation?

(1) a, only   (3) c

(2) b, only   (4) a and b

_____

<u>Aug '01, #13:</u> If n represents an odd number, which computation results in an answer that is an even number?

(1) $2 \times n + 1$ (3) $3 \times n - 2$

(2) $2 \times n - 1$ (4) $3 \times n + 1$

_____

<u>Aug '01, #15:</u> If $a + b$ is less than $c + d$, and $d + e$ is less than $a + b$, then e is

(1) less than c (3) less than d

(2) equal to c (4) greater than d

_____

<u>Aug '01, #20:</u> What is the smallest integer greater than 1 that is both the square of an integer and the cube of an integer?

(1) 8   (2) 0   (3) 16   (4) 64

_____

<u>June '02, #11:</u> Which is an irrational number?

(1) 0   (2) π (3) $-\dfrac{1}{3}$ (4) $\sqrt{9}$

_____

<u>Jan '02, #19:</u> Which is an irrational number?

(1) $\sqrt{9}$ (2) 3.14   (3) $\sqrt{3}$ (4) $\dfrac{3}{4}$

_____

<u>Aug '01, #29:</u> Ramon said that the set of integers is not closed for one of the basic operations (addition, subtraction, multiplication, or division). You want to show Ramon that his statement is correct.

For the operation for which the set of integers is not closed, write an example using:
- a positive even integer and a zero
- a positive and a negative even integer
- two negative even integers

Be sure to explain why each of your examples illustrates that the set of integers is not closed for that operation.

_____

_____

_____

_____

_____

<u>June '02, #24:</u> An addition table for a subset of real numbers is shown below. Which number is the identity element? Explain your answer.

+	0	1	2	3
0	0	1	2	3
1	1	2	3	4
2	2	3	4	0
3	3	4	0	1

_____

_____

<u>Jan '02, #13:</u> Which inequality is true if $x = \dfrac{3.04}{1.48}$, $y = 1.99 + 0.33$, and $z = (1.3)^3$?

(1) $y < z < x$ (3) $x < z < y$

(2) $y < x < z$ (4) $x < y < z$

_____

<u>Sample #4:</u> If $n-3$ is an even integer, what is the next larger consecutive even integer?

(1) $n-5$ (2) $n-1$ (3) $n+1$ (4) $n+2$

_____

<u>Aug '02, #22:</u> In the addition table for a subset of real numbers shown below, which number is the inverse of 3 ? Explain your answer.

$$
\begin{array}{c|cccc}
\oplus & 1 & 2 & 3 & 4 \\
\hline
1 & 2 & 3 & 4 & 1 \\
2 & 3 & 4 & 1 & 2 \\
3 & 4 & 1 & 2 & 3 \\
4 & 1 & 2 & 3 & 4 \\
\end{array}
$$

_____

_____

<u>Sample #13:</u> For what value of t is $\dfrac{1}{\sqrt{t}} < \sqrt{t} < t$ true?

(1) 1   (2) 0   (3) -1 (4) 4

<u>June '00, #3:</u> Which number is rational?

(1) π (2) $\dfrac{5}{4}$ (3) $\sqrt{7}$ (4) $\sqrt{\dfrac{3}{2}}$

<u>June '00, #11:</u> If $a \neq 0$ and the sum of x and $\dfrac{1}{a}$ is 0, then

(1) $x = a$ (2) $x = -a$ (3) $x = -\dfrac{1}{a}$ (4) $x = 1 - a$

<u>Jan '03, #14:</u> Which equation illustrates the multiplicative identity element?

(1) $x + 0 = x$ (2) $x - x = 0$ (3) $x \bullet \dfrac{1}{x} = 1$ (4) $x \bullet 1 = x$

June '03, #3: Which expression represents an irrational number?

(1) $\sqrt{2}$ 　　　　　(2) $\dfrac{1}{2}$ 　　　　　(3) 0.17 　　(4) 0

_____

June '03, #6: Tori computes the value of 8×95 in her head by thinking $8(100-5) = 8 \times 100 - 8 \times 5$. Which number property is she using?

(1) associative 　　　　(3) commutative

(2) distributive 　　　　(4) closure

_____

***_June '03, #14:_ If the expression $3 - 4^2 + \dfrac{6}{2}$ is evaluated, what would be done last?

(1) subtracting 　　(2) squaring 　　(3) adding 　　(4) dividing

_____

June '03, #15: What is the inverse of $\dfrac{2}{3}$?

(1) $-\dfrac{2}{3}$ 　　　(2) $\dfrac{1}{3}$ 　　　(3) $-\dfrac{3}{2}$ 　　　(4) $\dfrac{3}{2}$

_____

Jan '04, #28: Which equation illustrates the associative property of addition?

(1) $x + y = y + x$ 　　　　(3) $(3 + x) + y = 3 + (x + y)$

(2) $3(x + 2) = 3x + 6$ 　　　(4) $3 + x = 0$

_____

June '04, #13: Which property of real numbers is illustrated by the equation $-\sqrt{3} + \sqrt{3} = 0$?

(1) additive identity
(2) commutative property of addition
(3) associative property of addition
(4) additive inverse

_____

<u>June '04, #24</u>: Which expression is an example of the associative property?

(1) $(x + y) + z = x + (y + z)$
(2) $x + y + z = z + y + x$
(3) $x(y + z) = xy + xz$
(4) $x \bullet 1 = x$

_____

<u>Aug '08, #2</u>: The statement $2 + 0 = 2$ is an example of the use of which property of real numbers?

(1) associative   (3) additive inverse

(2) additive identity   (4) distributive

_____

<u>Jun '09, #26</u>: What is the additive inverse of the expression $a - b$?

(1) $a + b$ (2) $a - b$ (3) $-a + b$ (4) $-a - b$

_____

<u>Sample #5</u>: Which property is illustrated by the equation $ax + ay = a(x + y)$?

(1) associative   (3) distributive
(2) commutative   (4) identity

_____

<u>Jun '10, #32</u>: Perform the indicated operation: $-6(a - 7)$

State the name of the property used.

_____

Lists on the TI-73

If we want to do calculations on or graph a set of _____

_____ we can begin by entering the list on the calculator.

Press [LIST] .

The screen at the right should appear.

If one or more of the lists already contain data you should begin by clearing the list(s).

To clear one list it is easiest to press [▲] until

the list name is highlighted as it is in the screen at the

right. Then press [CLEAR] You should notice that

the numbers in the list don't change, but now the line

at the very bottom should be cleared.

Now press [▼] or [ENTER] . The list should be completely empty now.

A common mistake is to press [DEL] instead of [CLEAR] . Try it now and

see what happens: _____

_____

There are two ways to get the missing list back:

1. If you don't have any work that needs to be saved just reset the RAM. (See
    Appendix C)

2. If you do have work (lists, graphs, etc.) that

    you don't want to disappear, go to the

    catalog, [2ND] [PRGM]

    and scroll down until you find SetUpEditor.

    Press [ENTER] .

    You should be at the home screen now. Press [ENTER] again and the list along

with its contents should be back!

Correcting mistakes:

1. Forgot a number? It's not always important to have the data in a specific order – it might be okay to add it to the bottom of the list. Otherwise, place the cursor at the place you need the number to appear and insert the number. To insert, press  . A zero should appear in the list at this spot.

   Replace the zero with the number you missed.
   Practice now – enter the numbers 1, 3, 5, 7, and 9 in L1.
   Now make the list read 1,2,3,4,5,6,7,8,9 by inserting the missing even numbers.

2. Input the wrong number? Place the cursor on the incorrect entry and type the correct number over it.
3. Extra entry? Place the cursor on the entry you don't need and press [DEL]

Consider the following list of 15 quiz scores:
75, 80, 70, 90, 90, 95, 85, 60, 70, 65, 100, 90, 95, 80, 85

Enter the scores in List 1. Notice that your current entry stays on the bottom entry line until you press [ENTER] or [▼] to make it an "official entry" in your list.

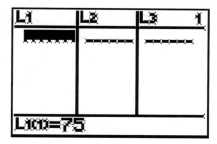

The number in parentheses tells you where you are in your list. After the last entry it should say L1(16) meaning that we filled 15 slots and its ready for #16.

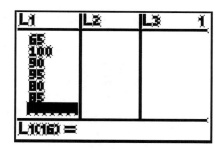

Once the list is made there are lots of things we can do with it. We'll start with something simple. To find some statistical measures like the median, you may have learned to put the numbers in order from least to greatest. The calculator can do this for you. Press [2ND] then [LIST] . Go over to OPS (operations) and choose 1:SortA(. The calculator should automatically go to the home screen. Note that whenever the calculator places beginning parentheses after an operation you MUST tell it what to perform that operation on. We want list 1 sorted so press [2ND] [LIST] again. This time choose 1:L1. Press [ENTER] at the home screen. The calculator will say

_____ .

Now you can go to the sorted list by pressing [LIST] .

You may have noticed that we choose Sort A as opposed to Sort D. "A" stands for

_____ and "D" stands for _____ . We wanted least

to greatest so we chose Sort A.

With some graphing calculators this is also the best way to find the _____.

Recall that the mode is

_____

_____

_____

With the numbers in order, any duplicates will be listed together and are easier to find.

The TI-73 will also find the mode for us.

Consider the set $\{25, 27, 39, 35, 24, 36, 45, 27, 34, 48, 24, 36, 41, 37, 26\}$.

1. Enter your data in a list.

2. Press [2ND] [LIST] (STAT). Use the arrow key to move the highlighted

    option to MATH.

3.   Choose 5:mode.

4. At the home screen you will need to tell the

    calculator which list to use. Press [2ND]

    [LIST] again. This time stay on the first menu,

    Ls, and choose the list your data is in. (Usually L1.)

```
mode(L1)
```

5. Close the parentheses and press [ENTER] .

6. The mode for our set of data is _____ .

Try this: Find the mode of the following set of data {-2, 6, 12, 3, 5}.

What happened?

_____

_____

Not all error messages require an action from you. This one occurred because there really

was no mode for this set of numbers. Just choose 1:Quit when you see this error and your

answer is _____ .

Is there a mode if every number appears the same number of times? Let's see what the calculator says.
Try finding the mode for this set on the calculator:

$$\{2,2,2,4,4,4,6,6,6,8,8,8\}$$

What happens?

_____

_____

What is your conclusion?

_____

_____

***Sources actually disagree about whether the calculator is correct in this case!!! For this reason, you will probably never be asked again to find the mode of a set of data like this.

Practice:

Find the mode(s) for each set of data below.

1. $\{5,10,15,10,25,0,5,20,15,25,35,30,35,25,15,5,10\}$

2. $\{0.1,0.01,0.01,0.1,0.001,0.01,0.1,.001,1.0,0.1,0.01,1.0\}$

3. $\{88,85,69,75,88,100,90,95,89,91,76,73,66,99,97,63,78,84,99,75\}$

4. $\{15,18,19,12,14,16,17,19,18,14,13,12,15,16,19,13,12,15,17,18,15,14,13,12\}$

5. $\{101,110,10,11,111,120,130,20,30,110,101,121,131,31,21,11,101\}$

Measures of Central Tendency

Recall that measures of central tendency are _____

_____

_____

We looked at mode in the last lesson. The calculator will also find the _____ and the _____ – in two different ways.

The first is very similar to the mode:

1. Enter your data in a list.

2. Press [2ND] [LIST] .

3. Use the arrow to go over to MATH.

4. You should see 3:mean(and 4:median(, choose the one you need by highlighting it and pressing [ENTER] or pressing 3 for mean or 4 for median.

5. You should be back at the home screen now. Input the list name and [ENTER]

The second method will find both at the same time. It will also give you a lot of other information about your data that you may or may not need.

1. Enter your data in a list.

2. Press [2ND] [LIST]

3. Use the arrow to go over to CALC.

4. Choose 1:1-Var Stats.

5. If your data is in list 1 just press [ENTER]

6. Otherwise, tell the calculator the name of the list you want it to find the measurements for.

7. Press [ENTER]

8. You will need to know the symbol for the mean to identify it in the list of measures that appears on the home screen. Look for _____ .

9. Look down the list of measures. You should see an arrow pointing down near the bottom left of your screen. The calculator listed so many measures that they don't all fit on the screen at once. If you scroll down using your down arrow does something look like it should stand for median?

_____ does stand for median. Some of the other measures will be covered in later lessons, others you won't need until future math courses.

Example:

Find the mean, median, and mode of the school administrators salaries listed below. (2007)

Source: http://www.emsc.nysed.gov/mgtserv/administrative-compensation/AdminCompensation52006.shtml

SOUTH JEFFERSON CSD	Superintendent of Schools	$102,214
ALEXANDRIA CSD	Superintendent of Schools	$108,602
INDIAN RIVER CSD	Superintendent of Schools	$136,048
INDIAN RIVER CSD	Assist Super For Instruction	$99,507
GENERAL BROWN CSD	Superintendent of Schools	$112,000
BELLEVILLE HENDERSON CSD	Superintendent of Schools	$100,320
SACKETS HARBOR CSD	Superintendent of Schools	$113,680
LYME CSD	Superintendent of Schools	$99,500
LA FARGEVILLE CSD	Superintendent of Schools	$114,759
WATERTOWN CITY SD	Superintendent of Schools	$146,013
WATERTOWN CITY SD	Assistant Superintendent Inst	$105,643
CARTHAGE CSD	Superintendent of Schools	$135,000
CARTHAGE CSD	Asst. Supt. Instruction	$104,025
CARTHAGE CSD	Asst. Supt. Business	$104,025
COPENHAGEN CSD	Superintendent of Schools	$101,766
HARRISVILLE CSD	Superintendent of Schools	$93,962
LOWVILLE ACAD & CSD	Superintendent of Schools	$117,859
SOUTH LEWIS CSD	Superintendent of Schools	$130,000
BEAVER RIVER CSD	Superintendent of Schools	$99,282

Enter the entire column at the right in List 1. The other columns are only for reference, you don't need to do anything with them. Try both methods. For some measures the second method is more reliable. For the measures we will want in Algebra, both methods should give the same result.

Mean: _____

Median: _____

Mode: _____

Practice:

Use the data in the table below to answer the questions that follow.

Life Expectancy at Birth for Selected Countries

Source: https://www.cia.gov/library/publications/the-world-factbook/fields/2102.html

Country	Male	Female
Brazil	74.57	76.38
Canada	76.98	83.86
China	71.13	74.82
Ethiopia	48.06	50.44
France	77.35	84
Germany	75.96	82.11
Haiti	55.35	58.75
Iraq	68.04	70.65
Japan	78.67	85.56
Malawi	43.35	42.61
Mexico	72.84	78.56
Mozambique	41.4	40.4
Singapore	79.21	84.59
United Kingdom	76.23	81.3
United States	75.15	80.97

1. What do the numbers in the table mean?

   _____

   _____

   _____

2. Find the mean, median, and mode for the male life expectancies.

   Mean: _____   Median: _____   Mode: _____

3. Find the mean, median, and mode for the female life expectancies.

   Mean: _____   Median: _____   Mode: _____

4. The life expectancies for the total population of the world are 63.89 years for males and 67.84 for females. Which of the measures found in #2 and 3 were closest to the world figures?_____

5. What is the difference between the mean life expectancy for males and for females in the countries listed above?

   _____

6. Did any of the figures above surprise you? _____ Explain.

_____

_____

7. Research:

    a. Locate the countries on a world map and mark their approximate locations below.

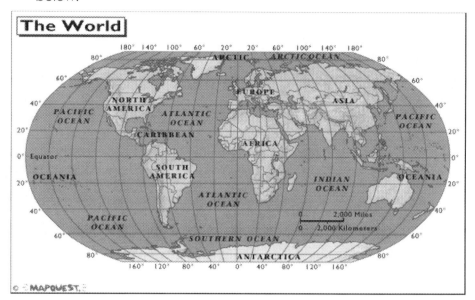

    b. Can you make any conclusions about the countries that have a low life expectancy compared to those that have a high life expectancy?

_____

_____

_____

_____

    c. Go to the website listed as the source of the data and check other countries to verify your conclusion. Record your results below:

_____

_____

_____

_____

    d. What factors contribute to the life expectancy of a particular population?

_____

_____

_____

_____

Range

Range can be interpreted differently in different contexts. For our purposes, range is

_____

_____

In the previous lesson, you learned how to use 1 Variable statistics (_____

_____) to

find the mean and median of a data set. In this same calculation there was a lot of

additional information that you didn't need at the time. Two of these measures can help

you to calculate the range.

The range is _____ minus _____, or the difference

between _____ and the _____

_____ .

> ***Although this is the only definition of range that you need in this course,
> later math courses will use another definition of range. The range in this lesson
> will continue to be the range you use for _____ .

**Remember – that means that the statistics range is

_____

Practice:

1. Go back to the School Administrators' Salaries on page 33 and find the Minimum, the Maximum, and the Range.

   Minimum: _____   Maximum: _____

   Range: _____

2. Go back to the Life Expectancy data on page 34.
   a. Find the range of life expectancies for males.

   _____

   b. Find the range of life expectancies for females.

   _____

Regents Connection

Measures of Central Tendency

_A.S.4a_

Aimee wants to buy a house. Houses in her community have recently sold for:

$125,000, $80,000, $140,000, $135,000, $136,000, $140,000 and $350,000 .

Given the above real estate information:
    What is the mean?

    What is the median?   _____

    What is the mode?   _____

    What is the range?   _____

                          _____

Using these different measures of central tendencies, explain which one is the best one to represent the cost of a house in Aimee's community.

_____

_____

_____

A.S.16a(Part 1)

In 2001 the city of Bedford Falls recorded the following number of sunny days in nine consecutive months:

                  5, 8, 15, 14, 11, 14, 8, 12, 8

Find the mean, median, mode and range for this set of data.

                              Mean: _____

                              Median: _____

                              Mode: _____

                              Range: _____

Jan '01, #18: From January 3 to January 7, Buffalo recorded the following daily high temperatures: 5°, 7°, 6°, 5°, and 7°. Which statement about the temperatures is true?

    (1) mean=median   (3) median=mode

    (2) mean=mode   (4) mean<median

                                                  _____

<u>Jan. '00, #5:</u> What was the median high temperature in Middletown during the 7-day period shown in the table below?

Daily High
Temperatures
in Middletown

Day	Temp
Sunday	68
Monday	73
Tuesday	73
Wednesday	75
Thursday	69
Friday	67
Saturday	63

(1) 69   (3) 73

(2) 70   (4) 75   _____

<u>Aug '00, #8:</u> On an English examination, two students received scores of 90, five students received 85, seven students received 75, and one student received 55. The average score on this examination was

(1) 75   (2) 76   (3) 77   (4) 79

_____

<u>Aug '99, #10:</u> On June 17, the temperature in New York City ranged from $90°$ to $99°$, while the temperature in Niagara Falls ranged from $60°$ to $69°$. The difference in the temperatures in these two cities must be between

(1) 20° and 30°   (3) 25° and 35°
(2) 20° and 40°   (4) 30° and 40°

_____

<u>Jan '03, #15:</u> The ages of five children in a family are $3,3,5,8,$ and 19. Which statement is true for this group of data?

(1) mode>mean   (3) median=mode

(2) mean>median   (4) median>mean

_____

<u>Aug '04, #2:</u> Rosario and Enrique are in the same mathematics class. On the first five tests, Rosario received scores of $78, 77, 64, 86,$ and 70. Enrique received scores of $90, 61, 79, 73,$ and 87. How much higher was Enrique's average than Rosario's average?

(1) 15 points   (3) 3 points

(2) 2 points   (4) 4 points

_____

<u>Aug '05, #1:</u> The weights of all the students in grade 9 are arranged from least to greatest. Which statistical measure separates the top half of this set of data from the bottom half?

(1) mean   (3) median

(2) mode   (4) average

_____

<u>Aug '05, #35:</u> Seth bought a used car that had been driven 20,000 miles. After he owned the car for 2 years, the total mileage of the car was 49,000 miles. Find the average number of miles he drove each month during those 2 years.

_____

<u>Jan '06, #18:</u> Melissa's test scores are $75, 83$, and 75. Which statement is true about this set of data?

(1) mean < mode   (3) mode = median

(2) mode < median   (4) mean = median

_____

Linear Transformations
Using Lists

The calculator can save some effort when performing a linear transformation on a large set of data.

Begin by entering the data in a list.

Example: Mrs. Zehr gives a test with 30 questions. She decides that each question will be worth 3 points and she will just give everyone 10 points so that the maximum grade will be 100.
We will let X be the set of raw scores (the set of how many questions each student answers correctly). Then we can write the linear equation $X' = 10 + 3X$ will tell us what the set of grades for the test will be.

Suppose $X = \{20, 29, 19, 10, 30, 25, 29, 18, 24, 22, 27, 21, 25, 30, 22, 26, 29, 23, 25, 27\}$ is the set of raw scores for one class. Enter these in L1.
Now move over to L2 and use the up arrow to highlight the very top of the list.

Now enter the expression for the transformation, but use L1 as the variable instead of X.

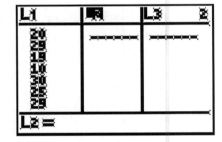

To find L1, press [2ND] [LIST] and choose 1:L1.

Now when you press [ENTER] List 2 should automatically fill with the transformed data.

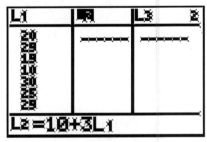

Scroll through the data to make sure it makes sense.
For example, in this exercise an entry greater than 100 would tell us that our formula might not be quite right.
Find the mean, median, mode, and range for each list.

List 1: Mean: _____   Median: _____   Mode: _____   Range: _____

List 2: Mean: _____   Median: _____   Mode: _____   Range: _____

What is the relationship between the statistical measures of the original list and the measures of the transformed list?

_____

_____

_____

Practice:

1. Mr. Hall gives a test with 23 questions.
    a. If each question is worth the same number of points, what is the maximum integral (integer) value that each question should be worth and how many points should be added to make the total 100?

    _____   _____

    b. Write an equation that will transform the number of questions answered correctly to a grade on a scale of 1 – 100.

    _____

    c. If $X = \{19, 22, 12, 15, 18, 19, 16, 23, 20, 19, 10, 14, 17, 22, 23, 16, 18\}$ is the set of the number of questions answered correctly by one class, find X'.

    _____

    _____

    d. Find the mean, median, and mode of X.

    Mean: _____   Median: _____   Mode: _____
    e. Find the mean, median, and mode of X'.

    Mean: _____   Median: _____   Mode: _____

2. Mrs. Homan gives a quiz with 6 questions on it.
    a. If each question is worth the same number of points, what is the maximum integral (integer) value that each question should be worth and how many points should be added to make the total 100?

    _____   _____

    b. Write an equation that will transform the number of questions answered correctly to a grade on a scale of 1 – 100.

    _____

    c. If $X = \{4, 6, 3, 4, 5, 6, 6, 4, 2, 3, 6, 5, 4, 3, 2, 1, 5, 6, 6, 3, 4, 6, 5\}$ is the set of the number of questions answered correctly by one class, find X'.

    _____

    _____

    d. Find the mean, median, and mode of X.

    Mean: _____   Median: _____   Mode: _____
    e. Find the mean, median, and mode of X'.

    Mean: _____   Median: _____   Mode: _____

3. Mr. Dunkel wants a conversion chart ready for his next quiz. If there are going to be 8 questions and each question must be worth a whole number of points, write a formula and use it on the list of numbers from 1 to 8 to fill in the conversion table below.

    Equation: _____

1	2	3	4	5	6	7	8

Regents Connection

Order Using Lists

You have seen these questions before, but now answer them by entering the choices in a list and sorting the list. Square roots, fractions, and π can all be entered just like any other value.

Neat trick: Any repeating single digit can be replaced by a fraction with that digit in the numerator and 9 in the denominator.

Jan '00, #2: Which number has the greatest value?

(1) $1\frac{2}{3}$ (2) $\sqrt{2}$ (3) $\frac{\pi}{2}$ (4) 1.5

_____

June '04, #33: Kyoko's mathematics teacher gave her the accompanying cards and asked her to arrange the cards in order from least to greatest. In what order should Kyoko arrange the cards?

_____   _____   _____   _____   _____

Let's Play Connect the Dots!

In this lesson you will get some practice naming coordinates on the Cartesian plane and create a picture on your TI-73.

Quick history lesson: Why do we call it the "Cartesian Plane"?

For thousands of years mathematicians never used graph paper and never plotted points. This frustrated Rene Descartes, a French mathematician and philosopher, because he couldn't explain how he knew that some mathematical ideas he had were true. So he devised the system of naming points as (x, y) coordinates. Descartes lived from 1596 until 1650.

Begin by creating a picture on the grid below using only straight lines. As you create your picture you cannot lift your pencil from the paper. You may retrace to backup but everything must be connected. As you draw you will need to fill in the table of values on the next page with the points that are the endpoints of your segments. You don't need to use the whole table if your drawing isn't that complex. Your goal should be to use at least 20 points. The more you use the better your drawing will look! You can estimate a decimal part of a value if your point does not lie exactly on a grid intersection.

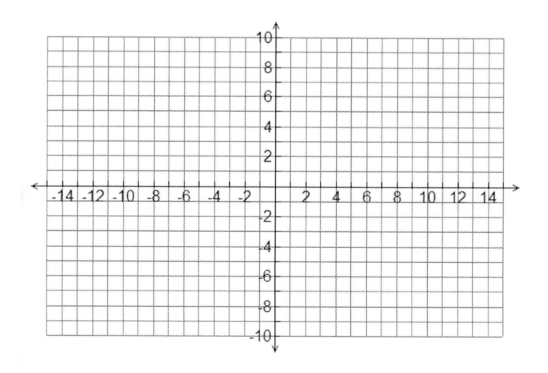

x	y

x	y

x	y

x	y

Now enter all of your x-values in L₁. Make sure you keep them in the right order!

Next we will make a _____ _____ .

Note that a "line graph" is not the same as the "graph of a line".

A line graph _____ _____ that are not
necessarily on the same straight line using _____ _____ .

To create a line graph press   .

Press on 1:Plot 1.
Turn Plot 1 on by moving the cursor over to ON and pressing .
Move down to Type: and move the cursor to the second choice.
It should look like a connected line.

Press   .
This will graph the line graph in the window the
calculator decides will show all of the data in the
best way.

**If there are some "extra" lines the first thing you should check is the Y= menu. Clear or
turn off any equations in Y= then press GRAPH to see if the problem is fixed. If not,
check your lists.

If your picture didn't turn out, practice on these smaller pictures. To complete the figure
be sure to use the first point twice, once at the beginning and once at the end to create a
segment connecting the last point back to the first.

1. $C(2,7)$, $A(-3,6)$, $T(-5,-3)$

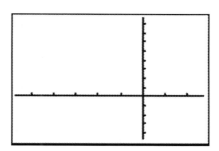

2. $M(1,0)$, $A(-2,-5)$, $T(-4,3)$, $H(2,5)$

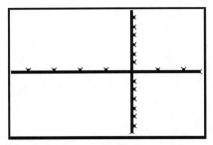

3. $P(-3,2)$, $Q(-6,6)$, $R(-6,1)$, $S(-3,6)$, $T(-8,4)$

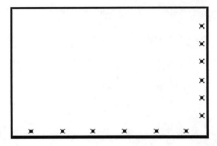

4. $A(3,3)$, $B(7,2)$, $C(6,4)$, $D(6,7)$

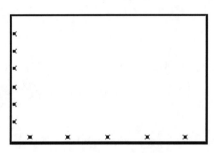

5. $U(2,2)$, $V(5,2)$, $W(6,4)$, $X(5,6)$, $Y(2,6)$, $Z(3,4)$

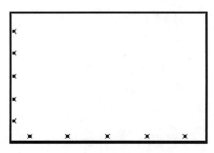

6. $B(-1,0)$, $U(-1,2)$, $T(-3,3)$, $E(-5,1)$, $R(-4,-1)$, $F(-1,0)$, $L(-5,-4)$, $Y(-5,-2)$

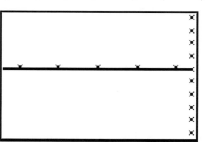

7. $F(-2,2)$, $L(-2,0)$, $O(-3,-1)$, $W(-1,-1)$, $E(-1,-3)$, $R(0,-2)$, $S(2,-2)$

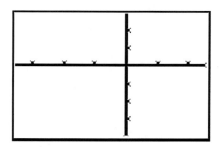

8. $T(0,0)$, $R(2,-5)$, $Y(6,-2)$

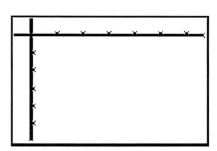

9. $T(1,1)$, $R(-1,1)$, $A(-3,-2)$, $P(3,-2)$

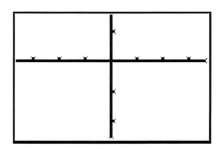

10. $S(1,-1)$, $T(0,2)$, $A(-1,-1)$, $R(1,1)$, $Y(-1,1)$

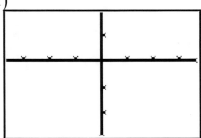

Evaluating Expressions

Recall that to evaluate means to _____

_____

We can use the TI-73 to help us evaluate expressions for given values of a variable.

Caution!! Be sure that you assign a value to the variable **FIRST, then enter the expression!!

All variables are assigned ZERO as a value until you give them a different value!

Let's start with an expression: $3x - 7$

Evaluate $3x - 7$ for $x = -8$.

1. Store -8 to x: **8**

2. Enter the expression $3x - 7$.

3. When you press   **ENTER**   the calculator will evaluate the expression for you.

Try these:

      A. Evaluate $2x - 9$ for $x = -2$.

      B. Evaluate $3x^2 - 10$ for $x = 3$.

      C. Evaluate $-4x + 7$ for $x = 7$.

Do we need to use x?

Any letter can be assigned a value; x is just the most convenient letter to use.

To use another letter begin in the same way but press   **2ND**   **MATH** , move

the cursor to the letter you want to use and press   **ENTER** , then use the arrow keys to move the cursor to DONE and press   **ENTER**   to return to the home screen.

```
A B C D E F G H I J
K L M N O P Q R S T
U V W X Y Z { } " _
= ≠ > ≥ < ≤ and or
        Done
N
```

Evaluate $4n - 12$ for $n = 11$.

      D. Evaluate $6c - 25$ for $c = 13$.

_____

_____

**Note – it is acceptable to continue to use x as your variable for convenience but be sure to use the given variable in your written work!!

This is especially useful for entering several different values into the same formula.

The formula to find the temperature in degrees Celsius if the degrees Fahrenheit is known is: $C = \dfrac{5}{9}(F - 32)$. If asked to fill in the chart below, begin by evaluating the expression for the first value given.

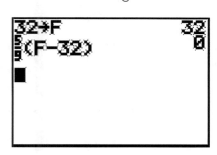

°C	°F
	32°
	50°
	70°
	80°
	100°
	225°
	350°
	400°

Store the next value to the variable. Then you can re-enter the formula or use the up arrow until the formula is highlighted and press ENTER.

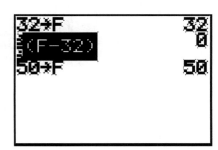

A new copy of the formula will appear on the entry line. Now press ENTER and the new value for the variable will be entered in the expression.

Complete the chart above.

Practice:

1. Evaluate $12x - 15$ for $x = 3$.

2. Evaluate $3m^2 - 5m + 12$ for $m = -2$.

3. Evaluate $-2y^2 + 7y - 10$ for $y = 5$.

4. Find the value of $5x^2 - 4y$ when $x = 3$ and $y = 5$.

5. Find the value of $5x - 12y^2$ when $x = 13$ and $y = -3$

6. The formula for changing Celsius temperature to Fahrenheit temperature is $F = \dfrac{9}{5}C + 32$. Use this formula to convert the Celsius temperatures in the chart below to Fahrenheit.

°C	°F
0°	
20°	
30°	
50°	
100°	

7. In Earth Science you use the formula $density = \dfrac{mass}{volume}$. Use this formula to find the densities of the substances in the table below. (Round to the nearest integer.)

Substance	Mass (in kg)	Volume (in cubic meters)	Density (in kg/cu.m)
Apples	1.5	0.00234	
Beeswax	2.3	0.00239	
Bran	1.1	0.00424	
Butter	1.5	0.00173	
Glass	3.5	0.00136	
Granite	5.2	0.00315	
Ivory	10	0.00543	

Regents Connection

Evaluating Expressions

A.CN.6c

Sarah wants to cover a cardboard box with plastic wrap. She is concerned that she does not have enough plastic wrap to completely cover the box. If the dimensions of the box are 9 inches wide, 4 inches high and 5 inches long, calculate how much plastic wrap she would need to cover the entire box, including the top and bottom. If Sarah filled the box with sand, how many cubic inches of sand would she need?

(Store values to L, W, and H)

$$SA = 2lw + 2lh + 2wh$$
$$V = lwh$$

_____

_____

A.N.6b

What is the value of the expression $(a+b)^2$ when $a = \dfrac{2}{3}$ and $b = -2$

_____

Jan '00, #15: If t=-3, then 3t²+5t+6 equals

    (1) --36   (2) −6   (3) 6   (4) 18

_____

Aug '99, #8: The formula $C = \dfrac{5}{9}(F - 32)$ can be used to find the Celsius temperature (C) for a given Fahrenheit temperature (F). What Celsius temperature is equal to a Fahrenheit temperature of 77°?

    (1) 8°   (2) 25°   (3) 45°   (4) 171°

_____

June '00, #21: the formula for changing Celsius (C) temperature to Fahrenheit (F) temperature is $F = \dfrac{9}{5}C + 32$. Calculate, to the nearest degree, the Fahrenheit temperature when the Celsius temperature is -8.

_____

Jan '04, #6: What is the value of $\dfrac{x^2 - 4y}{2}$, if $x = 4$ and $y = -3$?

    (1) −2   (2) 2   (3) 10   (4) 14

_____

June '04, #7: If the temperature in Buffalo is 23° Fahrenheit, what is the temperature in degrees Celsius? [Use the formula $C = \dfrac{5}{9}(F-32)$.]

_____

June '04, #32: Brett was given the problem: "Evaluate $2x^2 + 5$, when $x = 3$." Brett wrote that the answer was 41. Was Brett correct? Explain your answer.

_____

Aug '04, #8: If $x = -4$, and $y = 3$, what is the value of $x - 3y^2$?

(1) -13 (2) -23 (3) -31 (4) -85

_____

Aug' 08, #1: Which value of p is the solution of $5p - 1 = 2p + 20$?

(1) $\dfrac{19}{7}$ (2) $\dfrac{19}{3}$ (3) 3 (4) 7

_____

Jan '10, #10: The value of the expression $-|a - b|$ when $a = 7$ and $b = -3$ is

(1) -10 (2) 10 (3) -4 (4) 4

_____

Aug '09, #23: What is the value of the expression $|-5x + 12|$ when $x = 5$?

(1) -37 (2) -13 (3) 13 (4) 37

_____

Jan '09, #1: On a certain day in Toronto, Canada, the temperature was $15°$ Celsius (C). Using the formula $F = \dfrac{9}{5}C + 32$, Peter converts this temperature to degrees Fahrenheit (F). Which temperature represents $15°C$ in degrees Fahrenheit?

(1) -9 (2) 35 (3) 59 (4) 85

_____

Rounding

The TI-73 will round numbers to the nearest integer or a specified number of decimal places.

 Before we get started, a word of caution!!
Sometimes we need to use some common sense. For example, if our calculations show that we need 3.2 buses to take all of the students that are going on a field trip, we would need 4 buses so that everyone can go, although our rounding rules would tell us to round down.

With that said, many of you are likely already experts at rounding, but this exercise will give you a method to check your answers.

To use the TI-73 to round:

1. Press MATH

2. Use the ⟹ to move over to NUM.

3. Choose 2:round(

4. This action should return you to the home screen. Input the number you wish to round followed by a comma and the number of decimal places that should appear in your answer.

5. Press ENTER

Lets try a few:

a. Round $\frac{2}{3}$ to the nearest hundredth. _____

Hint: If you're unsure how many decimal places this is think of how many zeros are in the number one hundred. Since one hundred has two zeros, the hundredth's place is the second decimal place. How many decimal places would you need to be accurate to the nearest ten-thousandth?

_____

b. Round 9.45678 to the nearest integer. _____
(Remember, an integer has _____ decimal places!)
c. Round $14.23563 to the nearest cent then to the nearest dollar.

_____   _____

Practice:

Round each of the following to the designated number of decimal places:

1. $\dfrac{7}{9}$ to the nearest tenth.   _____

2. $\dfrac{5}{12}$ to the nearest hundredth.   _____

3. $32.1455 to the nearest cent.   _____

4. $315.67 to the nearest dollar.   _____

5. $436 \div 23$ to the nearest thousandth.   _____

6. $5241 \div 89$ to the nearest ten-thousandth.   _____

7. $57 \div 89$ to the nearest millionth.   _____

8. $719 \div 1200$ to the nearest billionth.   _____

9. $57,814 \div 27$ to the nearest billionth.   _____

   **Does the answer to #9 look correct? Knowing what you do about the calculator, what do you think the problem is?

   _____

   _____

10. What is the name of the most accurate decimal place possible to round to on the TI-73 assuming that there is no whole number part?

    _____

11. You and four friends place an order at Stefano's Pizzeria and agree to split the bill equally. If the bill came to $33.48. What is your share to the nearest cent?

    _____

12. Gas prices are posted to a thousandth of a dollar with all taxed already included. On a particular day the lowest local price for a gallon of unleaded gasoline in Lowville was $2.349. If Jay puts 10.8 gallons of gas in his car at this price, what will he be charged?

    _____

Fractions

Unlike many graphing calculators, the TI-73 has fraction keys.

Let's begin by reviewing some terms that we use when working with fractions.

A fraction is _____

_____

The number on top is called the _____ .

The number on the bottom is called the _____ .

A fraction that has a numerator less than the denominator is called a

_____ .

A fraction that has a numerator greater than or equal to the denominator is called

an _____ .

A mixed number is _____

_____

**Many textbooks refer to the number in front as the whole number part. Why is the definition above more accurate?

_____

_____

_____

***The calculator manual will refer to any fraction that is not expressed as a mixed number

as a _____ whether it is proper or not.

To enter simple fractions:
1. Begin by inputting the numerator on the homescreen.

2. Press $\boxed{\text{b/c}}$.

3. Input the denominator.

4. If it is necessary to enter other operations and/or fractions, use the right arrow to move out of the denominator before continuing.

Try these:

$$\frac{1}{3}+\frac{1}{2}= \underline{\hspace{2cm}} \qquad \frac{2}{7}-\frac{4}{5}= \underline{\hspace{2cm}} \qquad \frac{2}{5}\bullet\frac{2}{3}= \underline{\hspace{2cm}}$$

Now try $\dfrac{3}{4}+\dfrac{5}{8}$. You may have one of two possible answers. It should be either a mixed

number or an improper fraction. For now we would like mixed numbers. If your result was

an improper fraction, press MODE. The screen below should appear.

Using the arrow keys, move the flashing cursor to the 4th row down and press

ENTER with A∪b/c highlighted. This should make all of your results either proper

fractions or mixed numbers.

If you would like your results to appear as improper fractions you can convert them without changing the mode.

Let's start by entering a mixed number. To enter the number $5\dfrac{2}{3}$ on the calculator,

    1. Input 5 on the home screen.

    2. Press UNIT.

    3. Input the numerator and press b/c.

    4. Input the denominator.

To change this number to an improper fraction, press $A\dfrac{b}{c} \leftrightarrow \dfrac{d}{c}$ and ENTER.

What is $5\dfrac{2}{3}$ as an improper fraction? _____

To change a fraction to a decimal use $F \leftrightarrow D$.

What is $5\dfrac{2}{3}$ as a decimal? _____

Convert to a decimal:

1. $\dfrac{7}{8}$ _____   2. $\dfrac{4}{3}$ _____   3. $\dfrac{2}{9}$ _____

Use the same key to convert the following decimals to fractions:

4. 0.625 _____   5. 0.44 _____   6. 0.52 _____

Practice:

Express answers as both improper fractions and mixed numbers when possible.

Add.

7. $\dfrac{1}{3} + \dfrac{4}{5}$ _____

8. $\dfrac{2}{5} + \dfrac{7}{8}$ _____

9. $\dfrac{1}{7} + \dfrac{1}{11}$ _____

10. $\dfrac{4}{9} + \dfrac{6}{13}$ _____

11. $-2\dfrac{2}{5} + 3\dfrac{1}{9}$ _____

12. $1\dfrac{3}{4} + 4\dfrac{6}{7}$ _____

13. $4\dfrac{5}{8} + 6\dfrac{1}{6}$ _____

14. $-12\dfrac{3}{17} + 21\dfrac{1}{12}$ _____

$1/6 - 4\ 5/7$

Subtract.

15. $\dfrac{3}{4} - \dfrac{1}{8}$ _____

16. $\dfrac{2}{5} - \dfrac{1}{6}$ _____

17. $\dfrac{1}{9} - \dfrac{2}{3}$ _____

18. $\dfrac{2}{5} - \dfrac{5}{11}$ _____

19. $-2\dfrac{3}{5} - 1\dfrac{5}{7}$ _____

20. $5\dfrac{1}{10} - \dfrac{7}{8}$ _____

21. $1\dfrac{1}{6} - 3\dfrac{4}{13}$ _____

22. $-12\dfrac{3}{5} - 31\dfrac{5}{16}$ _____

Multiply.

23. $\dfrac{1}{6} * \dfrac{4}{5}$ _____

24. $\dfrac{2}{7} * \dfrac{4}{11}$ _____

25. $\dfrac{11}{13} * \dfrac{2}{19}$ _____

26. $\dfrac{3}{20} * \dfrac{4}{7}$ _____

27. $4\dfrac{1}{8} * 5\dfrac{2}{9}$ _____

28. $-7\dfrac{1}{3} * 10\dfrac{6}{7}$ _____

29. $11\dfrac{4}{9} * 4\dfrac{11}{15}$ _____

30. $20\dfrac{3}{8} * 5$ _____

Divide.

31. $\dfrac{3}{4} \div \dfrac{1}{7}$ _____

32. $\dfrac{5}{8} \div \dfrac{2}{3}$ _____

33. $\dfrac{1}{4} \div \dfrac{2}{7}$ _____

34. $\dfrac{4}{9} \div 7$ _____

35. $-2\dfrac{6}{7} \div \dfrac{1}{9}$ _____

36. $4\dfrac{2}{3} \div 1\dfrac{1}{11}$ _____

37. $4 \div 6\dfrac{3}{8}$ _____

38. $9\dfrac{5}{17} \div 15\dfrac{2}{5}$ _____

(Note: If one of these will not change to a mixed number for you, write the entire decimal you see on the screen.)

39. $\dfrac{1}{3} + 4\dfrac{4}{9} * 5\dfrac{1}{6} - 1\dfrac{2}{7} \div \dfrac{4}{13}$ _____

40. $2\dfrac{11}{23} - 1\dfrac{11}{19} * 33\dfrac{1}{18} + 14\dfrac{33}{34} \div 112\dfrac{1}{8}$ _____

Fractions in Lists

Fractions will also work in lists on the TI-73.

When might you want to change a whole list of fractions?

Let's start with a cookie recipe (these are a favorite with chocolate lovers!)

Chocolate Chocolate Chip Cookies

1	cup	Butter (softened)
$1\frac{1}{2}$	cup	Sugar
2		Eggs
$1\frac{1}{2}$	teaspoon	Vanilla Extract
1	teaspoon	Almond Extract
2	cup	Flour
$\frac{2}{3}$	cup	Cocoa
$\frac{3}{4}$	teaspoon	Baking Soda
$\frac{1}{4}$	teaspoon	Salt
2	cups	Chocolate Chips

Preheat oven to 350° F. In large bowl, beat butter, sugar, eggs, and vanilla until light and fluffy. Stir together flour, cocoa, baking soda and salt; add to butter mixture. Stir in chocolate chips. Drop by rounded teaspoonfuls onto an ungreased cookie sheet. Bake 8-10 minutes or just until set.

Makes about 50 cookies.

You have been asked to make 12 dozen for a bake sale. To find out how much of each ingredient you will need, enter the amounts in list 1.

What whole number should you multiply by to have enough cookies? _____

Use a transformation on the list to find the amount of each ingredient you will need.

Recall that to transform data from list 1, you can enter a formula in list 2. The formula you will want to use here is _____ .

Enter the new amounts in the recipe on the next page.

Chocolate Chocolate Chip Cookies

_____	cup	Butter (softened)
_____	cup	Sugar
_____		Eggs
_____	teaspoon	Vanilla Extract
_____	teaspoon	Almond Extract
_____	cup	Flour
_____	cup	Cocoa
_____	teaspoon	Baking Soda
_____	teaspoon	Salt
_____	cups	Chocolate Chips

Try it with this peanut butter cookie recipe. This recipe doesn't make very many cookies but it's my daughter's favorite so I often have to multiply it to fit the occasion.

Blue Ribbon Peanut Butter Cookies

½	cup	Shortening (or butter)
½	cup	Peanut Butter
½	cup	Granulated Sugar
½	cup	Brown Sugar
1		Egg
1 ¼	cups	Flour
½	teaspoon	Baking Powder
¾	teaspoon	Baking Soda
¼	teaspoon	Salt

Combine dry ingredients in a small bowl and set aside. Cream together the shortening, peanut butter, granulated sugar, and brown sugar. Mix in the egg and stir until well blended. Stir in the dry ingredients and chill for one hour.
Preheat oven to 375° F. Roll the dough into 1" balls and place on a cookie sheet. Flatten by pressing with a fork or with a cookie stamp sprayed with cooking spray and dipped in granulated sugar. Bake 10-12 minutes.

Makes about 2 dozen cookies.

Adjust the amounts to make 5 dozen.

_____	cup	Shortening (or butter)
_____	cup	Peanut Butter
_____	cup	Granulated Sugar
_____	cup	Brown Sugar
_____		Egg
_____	cups	Flour
_____	teaspoon	Baking Powder
_____	teaspoon	Baking Soda
_____	teaspoon	Salt

The Ice Cream Sundae Party!

You are having an ice cream sundae party for your class. You have decided on the recipes below and need to prepare enough for everyone in the class (PLUS YOUR TEACHER!) Use your TI-73 to multiply the amounts needed for recipes that do not make enough to feed everyone then prepare a grocery list.

I need to feed _____ people.

Chocolate Cherry Dessert Sauce

3/4 cup	Sugar
1/3 cup	Cocoa
1/8 t.	Salt
5 oz.	Evaporated milk
1/4 cup	Butter
1/2 t.	Vanilla
1/2 cup	Maraschino Cherries (Quartered)

In small saucepan stir together sugar, cocoa, and salt; stir in evaporated milk.
Add butter. Cook over medium heat, stirring constantly, until mixture comes
to a boil. Boil and stir one minute. Remove from heat; stir in extracts and cherries.
Makes 1 1/3 cup. (One serving = 2 Tablespoons = 1/8 cup)

Cocoa Brownies

1/2 cup	Shortening
1 cup	Sugar
2	Eggs
1 t.	Vanilla
2/3 cup	Flour
1/2 cup	Cocoa
1/2 t.	Baking Powder
1/2 t.	Salt

Heat oven to 350. Mix shortening, sugar, eggs, and vanilla until well blended.
Blend dry ingredients; mix in. Spread in well-greased pan, 8 x 8 x 2". Bake about 30
minutes then cool. Cut in 2" squares. (One serving = 1 2 x2 brownie.)

Butterscotch Topping

1 cup	Light Brown Sugar (firmly packed)
1/4 cup	Half-and-Half
2 T.	Butter
2 T.	Light Corn Syrup

Combine all ingredients in a heavy saucepan. Bring to a boil over medium heat, stirring occasionally. Makes 1 cup. (One serving = 2 Tablespoons = 1/8 cup)

Quick Vanilla Ice Cream

2	Eggs
1 cup	Sugar
2 3/4 cups	Half-and-Half
1 T	Vanilla Extract
1 cup	Whipping Cream

In a large bowl, beat eggs until thick and lemon colored. Beat in sugar until light and fluffy. Stir in half-and-half, vanilla and whipping cream. Pour into ice cream canister. Freeze in ice cream maker according to manufacturer's directions. Makes about 2 quarts. (One serving = ½ cup)

	Recipe will feed:	Need to multiply by:
Chocolate Cherry Dessert Sauce		
Cocoa Brownies		
Butterscotch Topping		
Quick Vanilla Ice Cream		

Adjusted Amounts:

Chocolate Cherry Dessert Sauce

_____	Sugar
_____	Cocoa
_____	Salt
_____	Evaporated milk
_____	Butter
_____	Vanilla
_____	Maraschino Cherries (Quartered)

Cocoa Brownies

_____Shortening

_____Sugar

_____Eggs

_____Vanilla

_____Flour

_____Cocoa

_____Baking Powder

_____Salt

Butterscotch Topping

_____Light Brown Sugar (firmly packed)

_____Half-and-Half

_____Butter

_____Light Corn Syrup

Quick Vanilla Ice Cream

Eggs

_____Sugar

_____Half-and-Half

_____Vanilla Extract

_____Whipping Cream

Be sure to combine amounts needed of the same ingredient from each recipe for your grocery list!

Grocery List:

Baking Powder	
Butter	
Cocoa	
Eggs	
Evaporated milk	
Flour	
Half-and-Half	
Light Brown Sugar (firmly packed)	
Light Corn Syrup	
Maraschino Cherries (Quartered)	
Salt	
Shortening	
Sugar	
Vanilla	
Whipping Cream	

Extension: Research how much each of the ingredients cost for each serving and find the total cost per person then compare with grocery store and restaurant prices.

Regents Connection

Fractions

A.N.5b

Theresa had 7½ gallons of fruit punch for her party. If half of the fruit punch was served, how many gallons of fruit punch did Theresa serve?

_____

A.PS.9a

Mario has a cookie shop. He has 30 pounds of butter and 60 pounds of sugar. A batch of butter cookies takes 6 pounds of butter and 10 pounds of sugar. A batch of chocolate chip cookies takes 5 pounds of butter and 12 pounds of sugar.

Determine which combinations of cookie batches he can make. Verify your answer.

3 batches of butter cookies and 2 batches of Chocolate Chip cookies

3 batches of butter cookies and 3 batches of Chocolate Chip cookies

6 batches of Chocolate Chip cookies

5 batches of Butter Cookies

1 of Butter and 5 of Chocolate Chip

What is the maximum amount of batches of Chocolate Chip cookies that Mario could make?

_____

_____

_____

_____

Aug '01, #14: In his will, a man leaves one-half of his money to his wife, one-half of what is then left to his older child, and one-half of what is then left to his younger child. His two cousins divide the remainder equally, each receiving $2,000. What was the total amount of money in the man's will?

(1) $40,000   (3) $24,000

(2) $32,000   (4) $16,000

_____

Aug '02, #28: There are 28 students in a mathematics class. If $\frac{1}{4}$ of the students are called to the guidance office, $\frac{1}{3}$ of the remaining students are called to the nurse, and, finally, $\frac{1}{2}$ of those left go to the library, how many students remain in the classroom?

_____

Sample #14: There are 12 tomato plants in a garden. Each plant has 7 branches and each branch has four (4) tomatoes growing on it. If one-third of the tomatoes are p cked, how many tomatoes were picked?

(1) 23   (2) 112   (3) 224   (4) 336

_____

Sample #16: Laura goes shopping. She spends one-fourth of her money on a pair of shorts, and one-third of her remaining money for a belt. If Laura has $42 left after these two purchases, how much money did she have when she started shopping?

(1) $84   (2) $126   (3) $144   (4) $504

_____

June '03, #28: In a town election, candidates A and B were running for mayor. There were 30,500 people eligible to vote, and $\frac{3}{4}$ of them actually voted. Candidate B received $\frac{1}{3}$ of the votes cast. How many people voted for candidate B? What percent of the votes cast, to the nearest tenth of a percent, did candidate A receive?

_____

Prime Numbers

A _____ _____ is an integer _____

_____ _____ whose only factors are _____ and

_____ .

Did you know that new prime numbers are found almost every year? As of the day this was written the largest known prime number is best written as $2^{32582657} - 1$ and if written out would contain 9808358 digits. This is more than ordinary computers can handle.

The current popular method to find new prime numbers is called GIMPS (the Great Internet Mersenne Prime Search). It uses the "down time" of tens of thousands of computers to search for the next "Mersenne Prime".

If you want to learn more about prime numbers and how they are found (and who Mersenne was) try http://primes.utm.edu/largest.html

In this lesson we will discover how to determine whether a number is _____ or _____ . And we will let the calculator find the prime factors of any numbers that turn out to be composite.

Another famous mathematician, Euclid (YOO-klihd), gave us the

_____

This theorem says that every positive integer greater than one can be expressed uniquely as a product of primes, (ignoring rearrangement of the same prime numbers).

When you are asked to find the prime factorization of a given number, this theorem says that we can find it and there is only one right answer.

How to do it:
1. Your calculator must have the mode settings displayed at the right so press

   MODE

2. Use the arrow keys so that "b/c" is highlighted, then press

   ENTER

3. Use the arrow keys again to highlight "Mansimp", then press **ENTER**

With the Mode correctly set, we will enter the number in question as both the numerator and the denominator of a fraction.

Let's try the number 47.

1. Input the number 47 on the home screen.

2. Press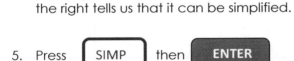

3. Input the number 47 again.

4. Press **ENTER** Your screen should

    look like the one at the right. The arrow pointing down in front of the fraction on the right tells us that it can be simplified.

5. Press **SIMP** then **ENTER**

6. The calculator simplifies the fraction and tells us the prime factor that it used to reduce the fraction. In this case it was 47. The same as the number we started with. This means that 47 IS PRIME!

Now we will try 144.

1. Repeat steps 1-5 above.

2. You should see the screen to the right.

3. The calculator divided out the number 2 and tells us that it can be reduced further.

4. Keep pressing **SIMP** and

    ENTER until the calculator displays $\frac{1}{1}$.

5. How many times did the calculator use 2 as a factor? _____

6. How many times did the calculator use 3 as a factor? _____

7. Then we can conclude that 144 is not prime and its prime factorization is

    _____ .

Practice:

For each number given, find whether the number is prime or composite. If it is composite find its prime factorization. If a large number gives an error message, write the message.

1. 59 _____ _____

2. 67 _____ _____

3. 81 _____ _____

4. 108 _____ _____

5. 131 _____ _____

6. 147 _____ _____

7. 151 _____ _____

8. 500 _____ _____

9. 745 _____ _____

10. 899 _____ _____

11. 1100 _____ _____

12. 1142 _____ _____

13. 1472 _____ _____

14. For large numbers that will not work can you find a method to "fix" the problem?

_____

_____

15. Try your method on any of the numbers above that gave you an error message and explain your results.

_____

_____

Percent

Although the TI-73 has a percent key, it is still important to understand how percent works.

Percent means _____ .

Sometimes we will still want to use the proportion method to solve a problem:

$$\frac{is}{of} = \frac{\%}{100}$$

We also may need to make some adjustments to the percent to make the problem easier.

1. When the question says "of" _____ .
2. When the question says "off" _____ .
3. When it involves a tax _____ .

To use the percent key on the TI-73 use the percent key after the percent has been entered on the homescreen.

Example 1: Find 15% of 60. (This question is looking for the _____ .)

Enter 15 [%] [X] 60 .   _____

Example 2: 35 is 20% of what number? (This question is looking for the _____ .)

Enter 35 [÷] 20 [%] .   _____

Example 3: 14 is what percent of 75? (This question is looking for the _____ .)

Enter 14 [÷] 75 [%] . $\left(\dfrac{is}{of}\right)$ _____

This finds the decimal $14/75$ and converts it to a percent.

Example 4: The regular price on a pair of sneakers is $\$69$. If they are on sale for 15% off the regular price and there is a tax of 8%, what is the final cost of the sneakers if they are purchased at the sale price?

_____

Practice:

1. Find 45% of 78.

2. Find 16% of 42.

3. Find 105% of 150.

4. Find 45% of 312.

5. 25 is 16% of what number?

6. 160 is 45% of what number?

7. 1220 is 240% of what number?

8. 450 is 35% of what number?

9. 85 is what percent of 145?

10. 412 is what percent of 500?

11. 1213 is what percent of 3000?

12. 8 is what percent of 42?

13. A sweater is on sale for 20% off the original price. If the original price is $62 what is the sale price?

14. The price of a laptop is $699. If sales tax is 8.5%, what is the total cost of the laptop?

15. 24 is 56% of what number?

16. What percent of 78 is 92?

17. A CD costs $19.95. If sales tax is 7.75%, what is the total cost of the CD?

Regents Connection

Percent

Jan '01, #22: Sue bought a picnic table on sale for 50% off the original price. The store charged her 10% tax and her final cost was $\$22.00$. What was the original price of the picnic table?

_____

Jan '00, #9: Twenty-five percent of 88 is the same as what percent of 22?

(1) $12\frac{1}{2}\%$ (3) 50%

(2) 40% (4) 100%

_____

Aug '99, #30: A painting that regularly sells for a price of $\$55$ is on sale for 20% off. The sales tax on the painting is 7%. Will the final total cost of the painting differ depending on whether the salesperson deducts the discount before adding the sales tax or takes the discount after computing the sum of the original price and the sales tax on $\$55$?

_____

June '99, #10: Linda paid $\$48$ for a jacket that was on sale for 25% of the original price. What was the original price of the jacket?

_____

June '01, #16: A boy got 50% of the questions on a test correct. If he had 10 questions correct out of the first 12, and $\frac{1}{4}$ of the remaining questions correct, how many questions were on the test?

(1) 16 (2) 24 (3) 26 (4) 28

_____

June '01, #27: A factory packs CD cases into cartons for a music company. Each carton is designed to hold $1,152$ CD cases. The Quality Control Unit in the factory expects an error of less than 5% over or under the desired packing number. What is the least number and the most number of CD cases that could be packed in a carton and still be acceptable to the Quality Control Unit?

_____

Aug '00, #29: After an ice storm, the following headlines were reported in the *Glacier County Times*:

 Monday: Ice Storm Devastates County – 8 out of every 10 homes lose electrical power
 Tuesday: Restoration Begins – Power restored to ½ of affected homes
 Wednesday: More Freezing Rain – Power lost by 20% of homes that had power on Tuesday

Based on these headlines, what fractional portion of homes in Glacier County had electrical power on Wednesday?

_____

June '02, #22: Ninety percent of the ninth grade students at Richbartville High School take algebra. If 180 ninth grade students take algebra, how many ninth grade students do not take algebra?

_____

June '02, #33: Mr. Perez owns a sneaker store. He bought 350 pairs of basketball sneakers and 150 pairs of soccer sneakers from the manufacturers for $62,500. He sold all the sneakers and made a 25% profit. If he sold the soccer sneakers for $130 per pair, how much did he charge for one pair of basketball sneakers?

_____

Aug '02, #25: In bowling leagues, some players are awarded extra points called their "handicap". The "handicap" in Anthony's league is 80% of the difference between 200 and the bowler's average. Anthony's average is 145. What is Anthony's "handicap"?

_____

Sample #33: A clothing store offers a 50% discount at the end of each week that an item remains unsold. Patrick wants to buy a shirt at the store and he says, "I've got a great idea! I'll wait two weeks, have 100% off, and get it for free!" Explain to your friend Patrick why he is incorrect and find the correct percent of discount on the original price of the shirt.

_____

Jan '03, #22: The world population was 4.2 billion people in 1982. The population in 1999 reached 6 billion. Find the percent of change from 1982 to 1999.

_____

<u>June '04, #20</u>: Rashawn bought a CD that cost $18.99 and paid $20.51, including sales tax. What was the rate of the sales tax?

    (1) 5%   (2) 2%   (3) 3%   (4) 8%

_____

<u>Aug '09, #35</u>: At the end of week one, a stock had increased in value from $5.75 a share to $7.50 a share. Find the percent of increase at the end of week one to the nearest tenth of a percent.

_____

At the end of week two, the same stock had decreased in value from $7.50 to $5.75. Is the percent of decrease at the end of week two the same as the percent of increase at the end of week one? Justify your answer.

_____

_____

<u>Jun '08, #35</u>: The Hudson Record Store is having a going-out-of –business sale. CDs normally sell for $18.00. During the first week of the sale, all CDs will sell for $15.00. Written as a fraction, what is the rate of discount?

_____

What is this rate expressed as a percent? Round your answer to the nearest hundredth of a percent.

_____

During the second week of the sale, the same CDs will be on sale for 25% off the original price. What is the price of a CD during the second week of the sale?

_____

Easy Box-and-Whisker Plots:

1. Enter data in L₁.
   Quiz Scores:
   78, 90, 85, 72, 100, 84, 60, 85, 95, 55, 75, 88, 97, 74, 77, 80, 92, 69, 75, 83

2. Press STAT

3. Move over to CALC

4. Choose 1:1-Var Stats

5. ENTER (Unless your data is not in List 1. If your data is not in List 1, you need to name the list you need the statistics for before pressing ENTER.)

6. If you need the mean, it is the first entry on the list.

7. Otherwise, scroll down until you see:

Minimum
First (or Lower) Quartile
Median
Third (or Upper) Quartile
Maximum

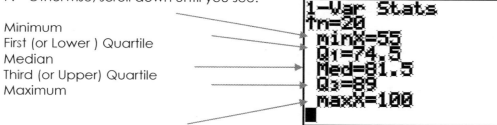

8. **The last five numbers are all you need and they are in the order that you need them.**
   Plot the minimum, first quartile, median, third quartile, and maximum just above the number line.

9. To find appropriate intervals, find the range of the data and divide by the number of intervals. Round up to a "nice" number. (i.e. a multiple of 2, 5, or 10 is usually easy to work with.)

10. Make vertical lines at the middle three points and make them into a box.

11. Make "whiskers" extending out to the min and max.

12. To check your work you can see what the plot should look like by creating a STAT PLOT.

    a. Press 2ⁿᵈ , Y=.

    b. Turn on Plot 1 (Pressing ENTER twice should do it unless it is already turned on.)

c. Use the arrow keys (Down then left or right.) to highlight the box-and-whisker plot. Be sure to choose the one with the vertical line inside the box at the median. Press ENTER.

d. Be sure the Xlist matches the list name where your data was entered.

e. Press ZOOM and choose 9:ZoomStat. This will automatically fit your data to the type of plot you have chosen. ***If an INVALID DIM Error occurs the list you have entered as the Xlist probably has no data. Check your list name.

Practice:

Create box-and-whisker plots on the next page using the data at the right and answer the questions that follow.

Selected States	Total Population in thousands	Total Participants in Wildlife Associated Recreation in thousands
Maine	966	511
Vermont	455	242
New Hampshire	887	448
Connecticut	2514	928
Massachusetts	4726	1835
Rhode Island	759	284
New York	13944	3800
Pennsylvania	9298	3886
New Jersey	6129	1864
Ohio	8522	6281
Virginia	5168	2278
West Virginia	1467	593
Maryland	3912	1537
Delaware	560	232

Source: U.S. Fish and Wildlife Service 1996 National Survey of Fishing Hunting, and Wildlife-Associated Recreation

1. Box-and-whisker plot for state populations:

2. Box-and-whisker plot for total participants:

3. Which set of data is more widely spread out, state populations in the northeast, or number of residents participating in wildlife-associated recreation? Justify your answer referring to the box-and-whisker plots.

_____

_____

_____

4. If the box part of the plot is narrow, we know that

_____

_____

_____

5. If the box part of the plot is wide, we know that

_____

_____

_____

6. Very long whiskers mean that

_____

_____

_____

7. Very short whiskers mean that

_____

_____

_____

Regents Connection

Box-and Whisker Plots
And Percentile Rank

A.PS.8c , A.S.9.a

The number of e-mails 20 different students sent in a week varied from 35 to 90, as seen in the box-and-whisker graph below:

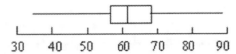

$$\begin{array}{ccccccc} 30 & 40 & 50 & 60 & 70 & 80 & 90 \end{array}$$

What is the minimum number of e-mails sent?

_____

What is the number at the 25th percentile?

_____

What is the number at the 50th percentile?

_____

What is the number of e-mails sent at the 75th percentile?

_____

What is the maximum number sent?

_____

A.CM.1e, , A.R.7b, A.S.5b

Draw a box-and-whisker plot for the ages of 13 employees at a local store:

21, 28, 29, 30, 31, 33, 34, 34, 37, 39, 40, 43, 57

A.CM.1f A.S.6a

Given the following ages: 20, 27, 28, 29, 30, 31, 33, 33, 37, 39 and 55

What is the minimum age?

_____

What is the lower quartile age?

_____

What is the median age?

_____

What is the upper quartile age?

_____

What is the maximum age?

_____

Construct a box-and-whisker plot for this data.

A.R.6b, A.S.11.a

The temperatures (Fahrenheit) in the first 20 days of March were the following degrees:

15, 25, 55, 38, 18, 39, 18, 45, 55, 61, 55, 18, 25, 17, 24, 35, 18, 25, 42, 43

Use this data set to identify the following:

Temperature at the 25th percentile.

Temperature at the 50th percentile.   _____

Temperature at the 75th percentile.   _____

What is the percentile rank of a temperature of 55 degrees?   _____

                                                       _____

June '02, #20: The accompanying diagram is an example of which type of graph?

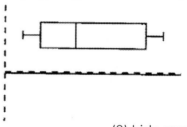

(1) bar graph   (3) histogram

(2) stem-and-leaf plot   (4) box-and-whisker plot

                                                       _____

Jan '03, #1: The accompanying diagram shows a box-and-whisker plot of student test scores on last year's Mathematics A midterm examination.

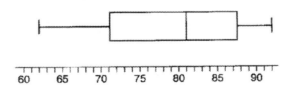

What is the median score?

    (1) 62   (2) 71   (3) 81   (4) 92

                                                       _____

June '06, #10: The accompanying box-and-whisker plot represents the scores earned on a science test.

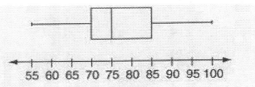

What is the median score?

    (1) 70   (2) 75   (3) 77   (4) 85

_____

Sample #9: The data set 5, 6, 7, 8, 9, 9, 10, 12, 14, 17, 17, 18, 19, 19 represents the number of hours spent on the Internet in a week by students in a mathematics class Which box-and-whisker plot represents the data?

(1)
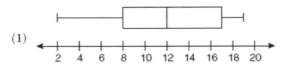

(2)
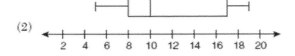

(3)
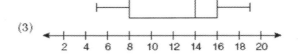

(4)
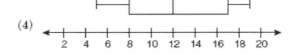

_____

Jan '10, #1: The box-and whisker plot below represents the math test scores of 20 students.

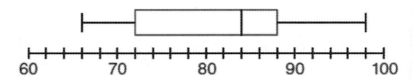

What percentage of the test scores are less than 72 ?

(1) 25   (2) 50   (3) 75   (4) 100

_____

Aug '09, #39: The test scores from Mrs. Gray's math class are shown below.

$$72, 73, 66, 71, 82, 85, 95, 85, 86, 89, 91, 92$$

Construct a box-and-whisker plot to display this data.

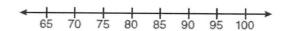

Jun '09, #15: The box-and-whisker plot below represents students' scores on a recent English test.

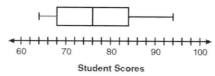

Student Scores

What is the value of the upper quartile?

(1) 68 (2) 76 (3) 84 (4) 94

Jan '09, #29: A movie theater recorded the number of tickets sold daily for a popular movie during the month of June. The box-and-whisker plot shown below represents the data for the number of tickets sold, in hundreds.

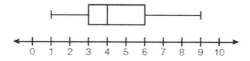

Which conclusion can be made using this plot?

  (1) The second quartile is 600.
  (2) The mean of the attendance is 600.
  (3) The range of the attendance is 300 and 600.
  (4) Twenty-five percent of the attendance is between 300 and 400.

Aug '08, #18: What is the value of the third quartile shown on the box-and-whisker plot below?

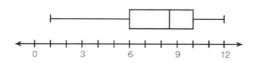

(1) 6 (2) 8.5 (3) 10 (4) 12

Statistics

Jan '10, #14: Which data table represents univariate data?

Side Length of a Square	Area of Square
2	4
3	9
4	16
5	25

(1)

Age Group	Frequency
20–29	9
30–39	7
40–49	10
50–59	4

(3)

Hours Worked	Pay
20	$160
25	$200
30	$240
35	$280

(2)

People	Number of Fingers
2	20
3	30
4	40
5	50

(4)

Jan '10, #35: Ms. Mosher recorded the math test scores of six students in the table below.

Student	Student Score
Andrew	72
John	80
George	85
Amber	93
Betty	78
Roberto	80

Determine the mean of the student scores, to the nearest tenth.

Determine the median of the student scores.

Describe the effect on the mean and the median if Ms. Mosher adds 5 bonus points to each of the six students' scores.

_____

_____

Aug '09, #10: Erica is conducting a survey about the proposed increase in the sports budget in the Hometown School District. Which survey method would likely contain the most bias?

> (1) Erica asks every third person entering the Hometown Grocery Store.
>
> (2) Erica asks every third person leaving the Hometown Shopping Mall this weekend.
>
> (3) Erica asks every fifth student entering Hometown High School on Monday morning.
>
> (4) Erica asks every fifth person leaving Saturday's Hometown High School football game.

Jun '09, #5: Which data set describes a situation that could be classified as qualitative?

> (1) the ages of the students in Ms. Marshall's Spanish class
>
> (2) the test scores of the students in Ms. Fitzgerald's class
>
> (3) the favorite ice cream flavor of each of Mr. Hayden's students
>
> (4) the heights of the players on the East High School basketball team

---

Jan '09, #7: Alex earned scores of $60, 74, 82, 87, 87,$ and 94 on his first six algebra tests. What is the relationship between the measures of central tendency of these scores?

> (1) median < mode < mean   (3) mode < median < mean
>
> (2) mean < mode < median   (4) mean < median < mode

Jan '09, #23: A survey is being conducted to determine which types of television programs people watch. Which survey and location combination would likely contain the most bias?

> (1) surveying 10 people who work in a sporting goods store
>
> (2) surveying the first 25 people who enter a grocery store
>
> (3) randomly surveying 50 people during the day in a mall
>
> (4) randomly surveying 75 people during the day in a clothing store

---

Aug '08, #4: Which statement is true about the data set $3, 4, 5, 6, 7, 7, 10$?

    (1) mean = mode   (3) mean = median

    (2) mean > mode   (4) mean < median

_____

Jun '08, #3: A school wants to add a coed soccer program. To determine student interest in the program, a survey will be taken. In order to get an unbiased sample, which group should the school survey?

    (1) every third student entering the building

    (2) every member of the varsity football team

    (3) every member in Ms. Zimmer's drama class

    (4) every student having a second-period French class

_____

Jun '08, #19: Which data set describes a situation that could be classified as qualitative?

    (1) the elevations of the five highest mountains in the world

    (2) the ages of presidents at the time of their inauguration

    (3) the opinions of students regarding school lunches

    (4) the shoe sizes of players on the basketball team

_____

Jun '08, #39: The prices of seven race cars sold last week are listed in the table below.

Price per Race Car	Number of Race Cars
$126,000	1
$140,000	2
$180,000	1
$400,000	2
$819,000	1

What is the mean value of these race cars, in dollars?

_____

What is the median value of these race cars, in dollars?

_____

State which of these measures of central tendency best represents the value of the seven race cars. Justify your answer.

_____

_____

Sample #7: Which situation describes a correlation that is not a causal relationship?

    (1) The rooster crows, and the sun rises.

    (2) The more miles driven, the more gasoline needed.

    (3) The more powerful the microwave, the faster the food cooks.

    (4) The faster the pace of a runner, the quicker the runner finishes.

_____

Sample #14: Which situation should be analyzed using bivariate data?

    (1) Ms. Saleem keeps a list of the amount of time her daughter spends on her social studies homework.

    (2) Mr. Benjamin tries to see if his students' shoe sizes are directly related to their heights.

    (3) Mr. DeStefan records his customer's best video game scores during the summer.

    (4) Mr. Chan keeps track of his daughter's algebra grades for the quarter.

_____

Sample #37: The values of 11 houses on Washington St. are shown in the table below.

Value per House	Number of Houses
$100,000	1
$175,000	5
$200,000	4
$700,000	1

Find the mean value of these houses in dollars.

Find the median value of these houses in dollars.

_____

State which measure of central tendency, the mean or the median, best represents the values of these 11 houses. Justify your answer.

_____

_____

Jun '10, #11: Which table does not show bivariate data?

(1)

Height (inches)	Weight (pounds)
39	50
48	70
60	90

(3)

Quiz Average	Frequency
70	12
80	15
90	6

(2)

Gallons	Miles Driven
15	300
20	400
25	500

(4)

Speed (mph)	Distance (miles)
40	80
50	120
55	150

Jun '10, #17: The freshman class held a canned food drive for 12 weeks. The results are summarized in the table below.

Canned Food Drive Results

Week	1	2	3	4	5	6	7	8	9	10	11	12
Number of Cans	20	35	32	45	58	46	28	23	31	79	65	62

Which number represents the second quartile of the number of cans of food collected?

(1) 29.5   (2) 30.5   (3) 40   (4) 60

Jun '10, #22: Four hundred licensed drivers participated in the math club's survey on driving habits. The table below shows the number of drivers surveyed in each age group.

Ages of People in Survey on Driving Habits

Age Group	Number of Drivers
16–25	150
26–35	129
36–45	33
46–55	57
56–65	31

Which statement best describes a conclusion based on the data in the table?

    (1) It may be biased because no one younger than 16 was surveyed.

    (2) It would be fair because many different age groups were surveyed.

    (3) It would be fair because the survey was conducted by the math club students.

    (4) It may be biased because the majority of drivers surveyed were in the younger age group.

Conversions on the TI-73

To convert from one unit of measure to another:

1. Enter the number of units you want converted. This can be 1 if you only need to know the conversion factor.

2. Press [2ND] then [UNIT] (CONVERT).

3. Choose the type of measure to be converted.
   Go to CONVERT now and write the choices for the type of measure below:

   1: _____

   2: _____

   3: _____

   4: _____

   5: _____

   6: _____

   7: _____

4. Choose the original units of measurement by pressing the number or highlighting

   your choice and pressing [ENTER]

5. Choose the unit you wish to convert to.

6. You should be back at the home screen. Press [ENTER] to complete the conversion.

What can we convert?

Under each type of measurement list the units available for conversion. Write the abbreviation or symbol as it appears on the calculator on the first blank, write the unit in words on the second blank. For the starred (**) blanks include the definition of the measure. Use other resources if necessary (dictionary, internet, etc.)

1. Length

1: _____ _____

2: _____ _____

3: _____ _____

4: _____ _____

5: _____ _____

6: _____ _____

7: _____ _____

8: _____ _____

2. Area

1: _____ _____

2: _____ _____

3: _____ _____

4: _____ _____

5: _____ _____

6: _____ _____

7: _____ _____

8: _____ _____

9: _____ _____

3. Volume

1: _____ _____

2: _____ _____

3: _____ _____

4: _____ _____

5: _____ _____

6: _____ _____

7: _____ _____

8: _____ _____

9: _____ _____

0: ** _____ _____

_____

A: ** _____ _____

_____

4. Time

1: _____ _____

2: _____ _____

3: _____ _____

4: _____

5: _____

6: _____

5. Temp

1: _____ _____

2: _____ _____

3: _____ _____

6. Mass/Weight

1: _____ _____

2: _____ _____

3: _____ _____

4: _____ _____

5: ** _____ _____

_____

7. Speed

1: _____ _____

2: _____ _____

3: _____ _____

4: _____ _____

5: ** _____ _____

_____

Practice: Converting Lengths

Answer each of the following questions using CONVERT on the TI-73:

1. How many feet are in one mile? _____

   **Although the question is worded "How many feet are in one mile?", you might want to think of it as "Given one mile, how many feet are there?". This may help you choose the correct order to enter the units in your calculator. The units of the given should always be entered first.

2. How many yards are in one mile? _____

3. How many inches are in one mile? _____

4. How many feet are in one meter? _____

5. How many kilometers are in one mile? _____

6. How many miles are in one kilometer? _____

7. An exchange student asks you how far from school you live.

   (a) Estimate how far this is in miles. _____

   (b) The exchange student doesn't understand this measure and asks you how far this is in kilometers. What should you answer?
   _____

8. True story: Climax Manufacturing Company in Lowville, NY makes many of the boxes you might receive gifts in. One of their machines is run by a computer program that measures in inches. Frequently adjustments need to be made with hand tools. These tools are made to measure in millimeters. The TI-73 was used to create a table for conversion. Part of this table appears below. Fill in the missing values. Measurements are made to the nearest thousandth inch.

Millimeters	Inches
1.4	
1.5	
1.6	
1.7	
1.8	

Other Conversion Practice:

1. A visitor from Canada believes that 90 km/hr is equivalent to 55 mph. If they are traveling 90 km/h on a road where the speed limit is 55 mph are they above, below, or at the speed limit? Give their actual speed to the nearest hundredth mile per hour.

    _____   _____

2. The Canadian visitors are now going to travel on Route 81 where the speed limit is 65 mph. What is the maximum speed in km/h that they should travel?

    _____

3. The maximum speed for boats traveling on the St. Lawrence River is 30 mph. How many knots is this?

    _____

4. Your punch bowl holds 14 quarts. How many liters of soda will it hold?

    _____

5. Is a US gallon larger or smaller than a UK gallon? How much?

    _____

    _____

    (What does UK stand for?

    _____)

6. John bought a building lot that is ¾ of an acre. He needs to know how many square yards this is to purchase the correct amount of grass seed. What is the area in square yards?

    _____

7. What is a hectare? Convert one hectare (ha) to some of the other area measurements until you find a likely relationship between them.

    _____

    _____

8. How many minutes are there in three weeks?

    _____

9. How many hours are there in a leap year?

    _____

10. How many centimeters long were you when you were born?

    _____

11. How many kilograms did you weigh when you were born?

    _____

Stem and Leaf Plots

Recall that a stem and leaf plot is

_____

_____

It is a picture of how data is _____ .

Consider the daily high temperatures for the month of September 2007 listed below:

71, 77, 79, 70, 74, 87, 92, 78, 62, 71, 69, 66, 71, 75, 57,
60, 67, 74, 78, 79, 80, 77, 68, 80, 86, 74, 64, 66, 64, 70

source: htt;://www.wunderground.com/weathersateion/WXDaily History.asp?ID=KNYWATER14 for
Watertown, NY

1. Enter all of the data in list 1 on your graphing calculator.
2. Sort the list from least to greatest.
3. As you scroll down the list note what numbers appear in the tens digits and write them on the blank provided.

   _____

4. The tens digits will be your _____ . Write them from least to greatest vertically on the stem-and-leaf plot below.
5. Go back to the list and write the ones digits as the _____ . Note that the leaves extend in a horizontal line after their corresponding stem.
6. Write the word "Stem" above your stems and the word "Leaves" above your leaves and give your plot a title.
7. The last step is to write a key. A key is important so that someone looking at your plot can be sure that your digits represent tens and ones. They could represent hundreds and tens, thousands and hundreds, etc. depending on the type of data but yours will usually be tens and ones.

Examples:

A key that reads $4\,|\,6 = 46$ tells the reader that when a 4 is placed on the left and a six on the right, it represents the number 46.

A key that reads $5\,|\,7 = 570$ tells the reader that when a 5 is placed on the left and a 7 on the right, it represents the number 570.

A key that reads $8\,|\,4 = 8400$ would tell the reader that

_____

_____

If the key says $6\,|\,2 = 620$, what number would $2\,|\,5$ represent?

_____

_____

What conclusion(s) can you make about the data based on the picture the stem-and-leaf plot provides?

_____

_____

_____

Practice:

1. Create a stem-and-leaf plot for the daily low temperatures in September 2007 listed below.
    52, 47, 56, 60, 48, 62, 73, 62, 54, 61, 55, 52, 45, 55, 44,
    37, 43, 48, 57, 59, 56, 68, 56, 60, 60, 66, 58, 51, 50, 49

2. Create a stem-and-leaf plot for the following test scores:
    89, 78, 90, 60, 87, 91, 100, 65, 78, 85, 87, 83,
    91, 96, 83, 87, 66, 75, 95, 88

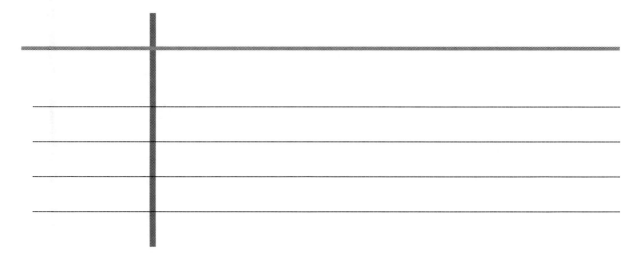

Stem and Leaf Plots

Jan '05, #35: Construct a stem-and-leaf plot listing the scores below in order from lowest to highest.

15, 25, 28, 32, 39, 40, 43, 26, 50, 75, 65, 19, 55, 72, 50

June '03, #21: The student scores on Mrs. Frederick's mathematics test are shown on the stem-and-leaf plot below.

```
4 | 3
6 | 0  5  5  7  9
7 | 2  5  6  8  9  9  9
9 | 0  1  2  5  9
```

Key: 4 | 3 = 43 points

Find the median of these scores.

June '05, #9: Jorge made the accompanying stem-and-leaf plot of the weights, in pounds, of each member of the wrestling team he was coaching.

Stem	Leaf						
10	9						
11							
12	3	8					
13	2	4	4	6	8		
14	1	3	5	5	9		
15	2	3	7	7	9		
16	1	3	7	8	8	8	9
17	3	8					

Key: 16 | 1 = 161

What is the mode of the weights?

(1) 145   (2) 150   (3) 152   (4) 168 1

Basic Graphing

We graph equations on the TI-73 by entering the equation in the _____

Press the [Y=] key. You should see a screen like the one below.

Notice that the equations are already started with "Y=" so any equation must be treated

as a _____ _____ and solve for _____ if

necessary.

If an equation uses letters other than x and y, replace the _____

_____ with _____ , and replace the _____

_____ with _____ .

If a statistics plot has been left on (like a box-and-whisker plot) you can tell from this screen. A stat plot left on will cause the name of the plot to be highlighted. The screen at the right shows that Plot 1 is ON.

These will interfere with our regular graphing so you should turn it off before continuing. It can be quickly turned off by using the up arrow to move the cursor to the top line and pressing enter while the cursor is flashing on the plot name that we wish to turn off.

Before going on, clear any existing equations (use the [CLEAR] key) and turn OFF any plots that may have been left on.

Resetting the calculator will also clear all equations and plots.

For this lesson we will want to graph in the _____ .

Your calculator may already be set to this window, but just to make sure, press [ZOOM] and choose 6:Zstandard. We look at the other options in a later lesson.

Examples:

Graph each equation on the TI-73 and sketch your screen in the space provided. Solve equations for y before graphing when necessary. Be aware that sketches must be labeled just like a regular graph and your line should cross the x- and y-axes at the correct values.

A. $y = x - 3$

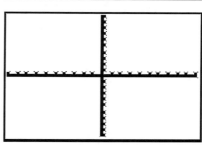

B. $2x - y = 3$

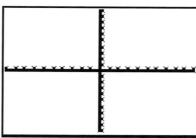

Practice:

Graph each equation on the TI-73 and sketch your screen in the space provided. Solve equations for y before graphing when necessary.

1. $y = 3x - 1$

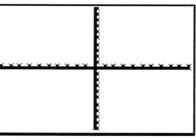

2. $y = -x + 5$

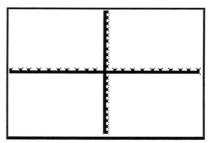

3. $y = -2x$

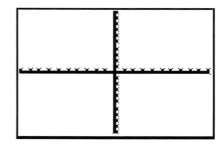

4. $q = -3p + 5$

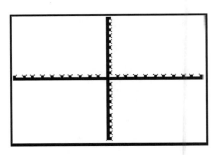

5. $m = \dfrac{2}{3}n - 4$

***Note that fraction keys work in the Y= menu.
The fractions will look slightly different.

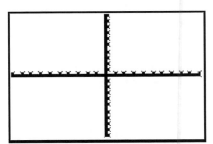

6. $y = -3\dfrac{1}{5}x + 2$

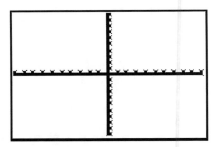

7. $5x - 3y = 9$

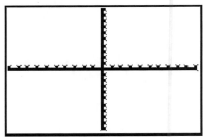

8. $-2x + 4y = -12$

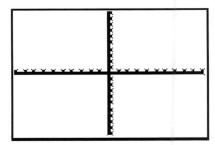

Windows

Just as looking out a window from different angles gives us a different view of the outside, changing the window on our TI-73 changes how we perceive the equation being graphed.

The "standard" dimensions are

$$Xmin = \underline{\hspace{3cm}}$$

$$Xmax = \underline{\hspace{3cm}}$$

$$\Delta X = \underline{\hspace{3cm}}$$

$$Xscl = \underline{\hspace{3cm}}$$

$$Ymin = \underline{\hspace{3cm}}$$

$$Ymax = \underline{\hspace{3cm}}$$

$$Yscl = \underline{\hspace{3cm}}$$

Xmin is _____

Xmax is _____

ΔX is _____

***** _____

_____

Xscl is _____

Ymin is _____

Ymax is _____

Yscl is _____

Describe the function graphed below:

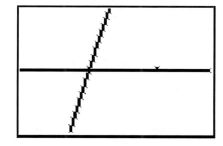

_____

_____

Now describe this graph:

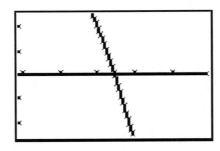

_____

_____

How about this one?

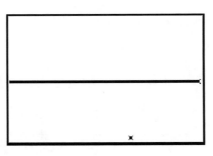

_____

_____

This is an example of how the window can fool you!!

All of these are actually different views of $y = -x^2 + 2x + 5$. Graph this equation in a standard window and sketch the graph in the "screen" provided.

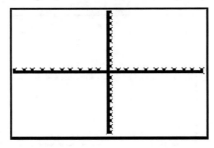

What is a better description of the graph of the equation?

_____

_____

So why is it important to use an _____ when graphing?

_____

_____

_____

Sometimes you will be told what part of the graph to look at. When this happens, begin by manually changing the window settings to exactly what you are asked to look at.
Example:

A. Graph $y = -5x + 15$ for $0 \le x \le 5$ and

$0 \le y \le 20$.

First change the window so that it matches the settings at the right.

**The ΔX should change automatically.

Enter the equation in Y₁ and GRAPH.

Sketch the graph in the space provided.

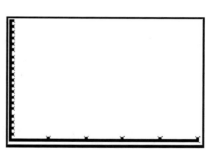

B. Recall that the x-intercept of the graph of an equation is

_____ and the y-intercept of

the graph of an equation is _____ .

Graph $y = \dfrac{12}{11}x - 12$ in a window that shows the x and y-intercepts. Sketch your

graph after you have adjusted the window and give your window dimensions.

Xmin= _____

Xmax= _____

Ymin= _____

Ymax= _____

Practice:

1. Graph $y = \frac{1}{3}x - 9$ for $0 \le x \le 40$ and

   $-10 \le y \le 10$.

   Change the xscl to 2. What difference does
   this make in the graph?

   _____

2. Graph $y = x + 16$ for $-20 \le x \le 10$ and $-10 \le y \le 20$ with xscl and yscl both equal

   to 2.

3. Graph $y = x + 8$ for $-10 \le x \le 5$ and $-5 \le y \le 10$ with xscl and yscl both

   equal to 1.

4. On the NYS math regents exams, if you use a scale other than 1, you must indicate
   your scale in some way. When using a sketch of a calculator screen, you are also
   required to indicate your window dimensions. Based on your answers to #2 and
   #3, why is it important to indicate your scale and window dimensions?

   _____

   _____

   _____

5. Graph $y = x + 17$ in a window that shows the x and y-intercepts. Sketch your graph after you have adjusted the window and give your window dimensions.

Xmin= _____

Xmax= _____

Ymin= _____

Ymax= _____

6. Graph $y = -2x + 25$ in a window that shows the x and y-intercepts. Sketch your graph after you have adjusted the window and give your window dimensions.

Xmin= _____

Xmax= _____

Ymin= _____

Ymax= _____

7. Graph $y = -\dfrac{1}{2}x - 12$ in a window that shows the x and y-intercepts. Sketch your graph after you have adjusted the window and give your window dimensions.

Xmin= _____

Xmax= _____

Ymin= _____

Ymax= _____

Troubleshooting

Things not working right no matter what you do?

Maybe one of these tips will straighten things out:

1. If you are trying to graph and the screen says:
You probably have incorrectly set your window so that the minX is larger than the maxX or the minY is larger than the maxY.

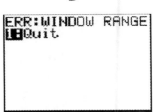

   This can also occur if you use _____

   instead of _____ when you change the window settings.

2. If the screen says:
You may be trying to graph something new, but have

   left a _____ turned on. Statistics

   plots will continue to graph until you turn them off,

   unless you no longer have the correct number of lists

   for them to create their plot from.

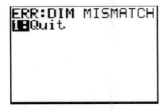

   You can tell if your plot is turned on by checking the

   _____. Note on the screen shot

   at the right that Plot1 is highlighted. This means it is on.

   To turn it off quickly, use the up arrow to go to the top line until Plot1 is flashing.
Press ENTER and it should turn off.

3. If you want your statistics plot to remain but get this

   error:

   You are probably graphing a plot that requires two

   lists and you have a different number of entries in

   each list.

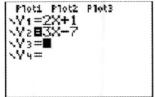

4. Your graph doesn't appear no matter what you change your window settings to.
You may have accidentally turned your equation off. If you press ENTER on the

   equal sign in the Y= screen, it turns the equation on or

   off. It is on when it is

   _____ .

   Which equation in the graph at the right is on?

   _____

Turning a function off can be a handy function if you want to keep an equation in the Y= editor but it makes your screen too confusing at the moment. Just remember to turn it back on.

5. If this error message appears:
    You have probably made an error entering your expression. The two most common causes of this error are

```
ERR:SYNTAX
1▪Quit
2:Goto
```

    a. _____
        _____
        _____
        _____

    b. _____
        _____
        _____
        _____

        Note that the Syntax Error was the first error we looked at that gave you an option other than _____ .

        If you choose _____ it will take you to where it thinks the mistake is. The calculator isn't always right, but it's a good place to start looking so that you can make the correction.

        Choosing Quit isn't usually very helpful!!

6. If nothing is appearing on your screen, your equation might just require unusual window settings.
    We will look at how to find these in later lessons.

7. Sometimes we have just made too many changes and we're a little lost. If nothing else helps, try _____ .

ZOOM!

In this lesson we will explore the changes that the choices in the Zoom menu can make in the appearance of your graph.

Begin by entering the following expressions in your Y= menu:

　　**Be very careful with your symbols and parentheses!

$$Y_1 = -\sqrt{\frac{1}{2} - x^2}$$

$$Y_2 = -\sqrt{5 - x^2}$$

$$Y_3 = \sqrt{\frac{1}{2} - (x - 2)^2} + 1$$

$$Y_4 = \sqrt{\frac{1}{2} - (x + 2)^2} + 1$$

So that we all start with the same window, we will begin with Zoom Standard.

Press [ZOOM] and choose 6:Zstandard. You should now be at the graphing screen. Sketch your graph in the space provided.

It should resemble a face – at least with eyes, nose, and mouth.

Before we look at more zoom options let's take a look at format choices.

Press [2ND] [ZOOM] .

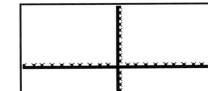

The screen should look like the one at the right.

The first and last choices only apply when tracing which we will look at later. (You will probably always want them on.)

Try moving the cursor from GridOff to GridOn, press [ENTER] then [GRAPH] . How did this change the appearance of your screen?

_____

_____

Go back to the Format menu and return the setting to GridOff. Now change LabelOff to LabelOn. How does this change the appearance of the graph?

_____

Go back to the Format menu. Leave the LabelOn but now turn the AxesOff. Sketch your screen as it appears now.

Note that when we turned the axes off the calculator assumed that the label was no longer necessary.

***As we try different zoom options. be sure to go back to a standard window between each choice to see its full effect.

1. Try 1:ZBox. At first this will appear to have no effect accept to put a flashing point on our nose. Press [ENTER] . Move the cursor up then right using the arrow keys. A box should appear on your screen. When the "eye" has been enclosed by your box, press [ENTER] . Sketch your screen.

(Remember to always Zoom 6 before going to the next zoom choice!!)

2. Now try 2:Zoom In. Again, nothing happens at first. Press ENTER once and sketch your screen.

Press ENTER again. What happens?

---

3. Now 3:Zoom Out, press ENTER once and sketch your screen.

4. Now 4:ZQuadrant 1.

5. How about 5:ZSquare?

6. Try 8:ZDecimal.

7. Now 9:ZoomFit.

8. You may have noticed that we skipped a few choices.
   a. ZoomStat will only apply when a plot has been turned on. It will choose the best window based on the type of plot and the magnitude of the values in the lists.
   b. ZInteger will do basically what Zoom Standard does but you can move the center point.
   c. ZTrig will not make any change unless a trigonometric function has been entered (sine, cosine, or tangent). Since we will not need to graph these until Algebra 2 we will save it for later.

The original equations you were asked to graph were intended to be ½ circles. Which choices made them look most like circles?

_____

_____ and _____ are both good

choices if you want your graph to be _____correctly.

You may have notices MEMORY at the top of the ZOOM menu screen.

After you press [ZOOM]   use the right arrow to move over to MEMORY and press

[ENTER] .

1:Zprevious will _____

2: SetFactors will _____

_____

You will probably not need to use these unless you want to increase or decrease how fast you zoom in or out.

Be sure to return your Format settings so that the Axes are On!!

Table and Trace

Once we have an expression entered in the Y = menu, there are some more things we can do.

In this lesson we will look at two more ways that we can use the TI-73 to evaluate expressions.

Begin by entering $3x - 7$ in Y1.

If we want to evaluate at several integer values of x it is probably quickest to use the

_____ .

Press   . Your screen should

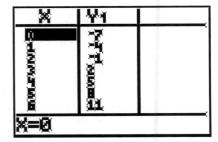

look similar to the one at the right. Your X and Y1 lists

may start at different values.

If you want see values other than the ones shown, use the up and down arrows.

**Note that the up arrow will not work in the Y1 list but the down arrow will. Either will work in the X list.

This is fine if we want a value just off the screen in either direction, but what if we need to evaluate the expression for $x = 100$?

Yes we can just hold the down arrow down until we get there, but there is a quicker way.

Press $\boxed{2^{ND}}$ $\boxed{\text{WINDOW}}$.

Where it says "TblStart = " input the value you want to evaluate the expression at.

This will move this x -value to the top of the table.

Try it now. Evaluate the expression we entered for the following values:

1. $x = 100$ _____

2. $x = 1,000$ _____
   (Do not include the comma when entering numbers greater than or equal to 1000!)

3. $x = 10,000$ _____

What happens if we try this with $x = 1,000,000$? _____

This happens when the number in the list is too wide for the column. The calculator has converted the number to scientific notation (which we will look at more closely later). Note that you can still see the exact value at the bottom of the screen.

Evaluate the expression at $x = 1,000,005$. Move down the X column watching the bottom of the screen until you get to 1,000,005. Then move the cursor over to the Y1 column to get the exact value for Y.

_____

We can also set the table so that it gives us exactly the x-values that we ask for.

Go to Table Set again and you should see near the bottom of the screen

Indpnt: Auto Ask
Depend: Auto Ask

Indpnt stands for the _____ which is _____ .

Depend stands for the _____ which is _____ .

If we change the independent variable to Ask, we can make a table of only the x-values that we wish to look at.

Note that we cannot choose for the dependent variable to be set at Ask without the independent variable to be set at Ask. It is best to leave the dependent variable on Auto.

Try it now.
Complete the table below by generating the same table of x-values on the calculator. (Yes you can enter fractions in the table!)

X	Y1
-2.5	
-1.25	
0.6	
3.75	
1/6	

If we only need one or two values, we may want to use _____ instead.

Graph the equation in a standard window.

Press [TRACE] .

You should notice that the
_____ appears in the upper left corner. The position of the cursor is indicated at the bottom of the screen. For x-values **in the current window**, you can just input the number at this stage.

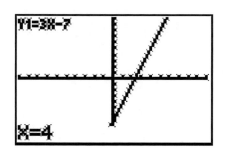

Try $x = 4$ (just press the number 4)

Then press [ENTER] .

The cursor will move to this x-value and tell you the value for y.

Y= _____

What happens if we try $x = 20$? _____

In order to use Trace you would need to change your window settings.

Practice:

Complete the following using whichever method is more efficient.

1. Evaluate $y = 4x - 12$ at each of the following values:

   a. $x = 6$ _____

   b. $x = 15$ _____

   c. $x = 100$ _____

2. Complete the table below for $y = \dfrac{1}{2}x + 20$.

X	Y1
-25.5	
-14.8	
1.2	
3 1/8	
11 1/9	

3. Evaluate $y = -\dfrac{2}{3}x + 7$ at each of the following values:

   a. $x = -2$ _____

   b. $x = -1.5$ _____

   c. $x = \dfrac{4}{9}$ _____

4. Evaluate $y = 150x - 24{,}000$ at each of the following values:

   a. $x = 100$ _____

   b. $x = 1{,}000$ _____

   c. $x = 1{,}000{,}000$ _____

5. Evaluate $y = -\dfrac{11}{9}x + 170$ for each of the following values:

    a. $x = 100$ _____

    b. $x = 500$ _____

    c. $x = 10,000$ _____

    d. $x = 1,000,000$ _____

    e. $x = 1,000,011$ _____

6. Complete the following table for $y = -2\dfrac{7}{9}x + 5\dfrac{1}{12}$:

X	Y1
-3 1/9	
-2 2/3	
π	
12 3/5	
25 1/7	

7. Complete the following table for $y = -3x + \dfrac{15}{22}$:

X	Y1
-4 1/4	
-1 7/8	
-0.86	
25 2/3	
100 1/3	

8. Write an equation that will find the circumference, y, of a circle with diameter x.

                                                       _____

    Use your equation to find the circumference of circles with:

        a. Diameter = 5   _____

        b. Radius =   15   _____

        c. Radius =   9   _____

        d. Diameter = 10   _____

        e. Diameter = 20   _____

Histograms

Histograms are a common way to display data that can be grouped into _____ .

There are two types of histograms, _____ and

_____ .

Consider the test scores for Test 1 in Integrated Algebra:

> 48, 92, 93, 86, 62, 78, 66, 66, 90, 90, 90, 50, 67, 95, 90, 98, 90, 100,
> 70, 77, 100, 54, 27, 89, 95, 100, 98, 88, 83, 73, 90, 77, 78, 64, 82,
> 61, 75, 95, 82, 90, 74, 93, 19, 90, 94

Begin by entering the data in L1.
Sort list 1.
Complete the table below:

To find the frequency, _____ .

To find the cumulative frequency,

_____

_____ .

Notice that the intervals begin at _____ and do not _____ .

The intervals are all the _____ , in this case they are all _____ .

Interval	Frequency	Cumulative Frequency
0-9		
10-19		
20-29		
30-39		
40-49		
50-59		
60-69		
70-79		
80-89		
90-99		
100-109		

Create a properly labeled **frequency** histogram of the test scores on the grid below.

Proper labeling means that

1. _____

_____

2. _____

_____

3. _____

_____

4. _____

_____

5. _____

_____

Create a **cumulative frequency** histogram of the test scores below. Label appropriately!

The cumulative frequency histogram

1. _____

_____

2. _____

_____

3. _____

_____

If you were given only the frequency histogram, how could you tell how many students took the test? _____

If you were given only the cumulative frequency histogram, how could you tell how many students took the test? _____

_____

To check your frequency histogram you can plot the graph on the graphing calculator.

1. Press [2ND] [Y=] (Stat Plot).

2. Press [ENTER] .

3. Using the arrow keys highlight ON and press [ENTER] .

4.   Highlight the picture of the type of graph

     we want and press [ENTER] .

5.   Be sure it says L₁ after Xlist:

6. Press [GRAPH] .

7.   The default screen will probably not give the best view (if any)

     of the data. To see a better graph, press [ZOOM] , choose **7:ZoomStat**. Now the

     calculator will adjust the screen based on the type of plot you have chosen and

     the range of data.

8. Sketch the screen in the box below.

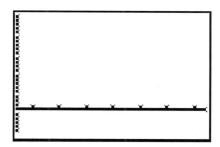

Does the screen match the graph you made earlier? _____

Press [WINDOW] . Your screen should look like the one below.

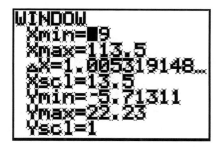

The calculator has decided where to begin (Xmin) and the size of the intervals (Xscl). Who ever heard of a histogram with intervals of 13.5?!!

Easily changed! **With the cursor on Xmin enter 0**. Then **with the cursor on Xscl enter 10** so that it now looks like the screen below.

Now press [GRAPH] . Does your graph look like the one below?

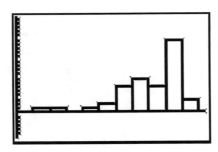

To check the intervals and frequency press [TRACE] and use the left and right arrow keys. The values on the screen below tell us that the cursor is in the interval 70 - 79 and the frequency for this interval is 8 .

In the upper corner we can see that we are in P1 (plot 1) and is created using data from L1 (list 1).

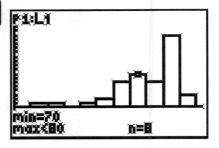

Why did we make the xscl = 10 ? _____

_____

Because we cannot make our intervals of different sizes, we cannot make a cumulative frequency histogram on the TI-73.

Although it didn't matter in this example, sometimes changing the size of the interval creates one or more intervals that are too large for the screen. Be sure that the _____ is larger than the most data contained in any particular interval.

The Ymin should be left negative so that

_____

Practice:

1. Make a frequency histogram on the TI-73 for the following data:

    Quiz scores: 75, 95, 78, 90, 75, 86, 84, 88, 92, 96, 100, 55, 70, 68,
    90, 92, 78, 80, 70, 92, 85, 88, 72, 80, 82, 90, 100, 65,
    76, 88, 86, 80, 100, 65, 75, 95, 85, 80, 68, 75, 100, 90

    ***Make 50 the xmin but indicate the break in values! Label as you would
    on graph paper.

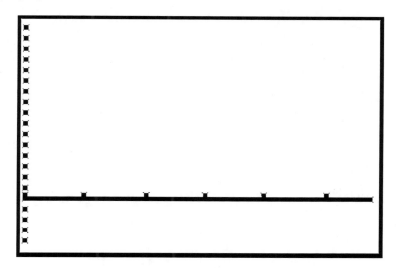

2. Make a frequency histogram from the following set of data:

    Temperatures in January in Degrees Fahrenheit:
    30, 22, 14, 10, 20, 28, 34, 36, 39, 29, 20, 12, 8, -2, -10,-15, -8,
    0, 5, 12, 18, 24, 10, -5, 0, 15, 30, 35, 25, 26, 34

    Change the xmin to −20 and the xscl to 10.

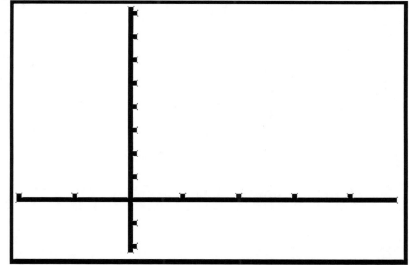

3. Given the frequency histogram below, create a cumulative frequency histogram of the same data.

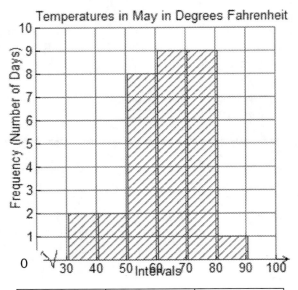

Temperatures in May in Degrees Fahrenheit

Interval	Frequency	Cumulative Frequency

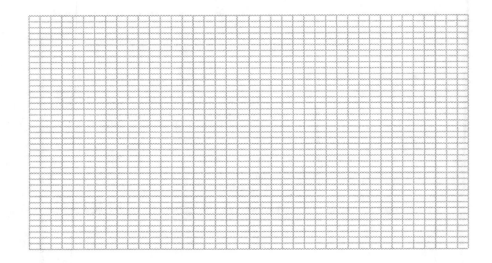

Regents Connection

Histograms

A.CM.1d, A.R.7a, A.S.5a
A police officer was studying traffic patterns in one part of town. In this study he recorded the speeds of 17 cars traveling in a 40 mph zone.

Here are the speeds in miles per hour:
35, 40, 42, 43, 45, 46, 37, 38, 52, 39, 47, 42, 41, 39, 54, 52, and 25.

Construct a histogram and a cumulative frequency histogram for this data.
(For the histogram, use the intervals 21-25, 26-30, 31-35, 36-40, 41-45, 46-50 and 51-55. For the cumulative frequency histogram, use the intervals 21-25, 21-30, 21-35, 21-40, 21-45, 21-50 and 21-55.)

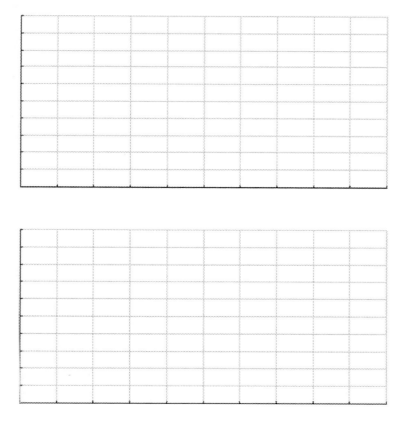

_A.PS.8d, A.S.9.b_

Mathematics Test Scores of Mr. Smith's Class

Interval (Test Scores)	Cumulative Frequency (Number)
60-100	101
60-95	100
60-90	69
60-85	35
60-80	20
60-75	8
60-70	5
60-65	2

How many students in Mr. Smith's class scored greater than an 85 ?

How many students scored at least a 66, but no more than an 85 ?

Jan '01, #32: On a science quiz, 20 students received the following scores: 100, 95, 95, 90, 85, 85, 85, 80, 80, 80, 80, 75, 75, 75, 70, 70, 65, 65, 60, 55.
Construct a statistical graph, such as a histogram or a stem-and-leaf plot, to display this data. [Be sure to title the graph and label all axes or parts used.]

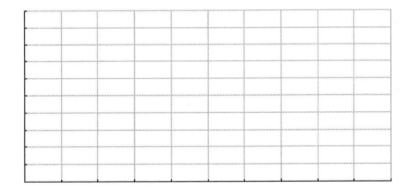

<u>Aug '01, #34:</u> The following data consists of the weights, in pounds, of 30 adults:

195, 206, 100, 98, 150, 210, 195, 106, 195, 168, 180, 212, 104, 195, 100, 216, 195, 209, 112, 99, 206, 116, 195, 100, 142, 100, 135, 98, 160, 155

Using the data, complete the accompanying cumulative frequency table and construct a cumulative frequency histogram on the grid below.

Interval	Frequency	Cumulative Frequency
51-100		
101-150		
151-200		
201-250		

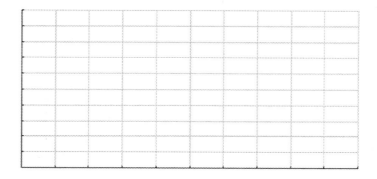

<u>June '00, #33:</u> The scores on a mathematics test were 70, 55, 61, 80, 85, 72, 65, 40, 74, 68, and 84. Complete the accompanying table, and use the table to construct a frequency histogram for these scores.

Score	Tally	Frequency
40-49		
50-59		
60-69		
70-79		
80-89		

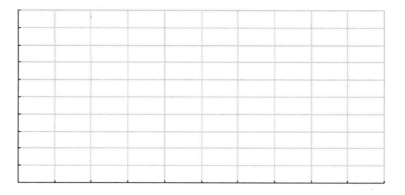

<u>Jan '00, #32:</u> In the time trials for the 400-meter run at the state sectionals, the 15 runners recorded the times shown in the table below.

400-Meter Run

Time (sec)	Frequency
50.0-50.9	
51.0-51.9	I I
52.0-52.9	I I I I I
53.0-53.9	I I I
54.0-54.9	I I I I

a. Using the data from the frequency column, draw a frequency histogram on the grid provided below.

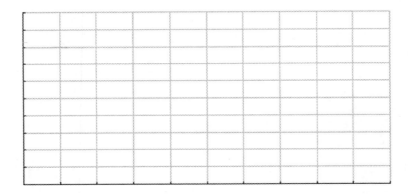

b. What percent of the runners completed the time trial between 52.0 and 53.9 seconds?

_____

<u>Math A Sample #18:</u> The accompanying histogram shows the scores of students on a Math A test.

Cumulative Frequency Histogram

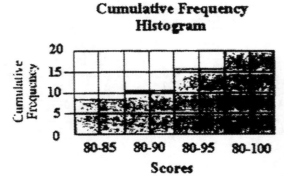

How many students have scores of 96 to 100?

(1) 55   (2) 20   (3) 5   (4) 4

_____

<u>Jan '03, #34:</u> Sarah's mathematics grades for one marking period were 85, 72, 97, 81, 77, 93, 100, 75, 86, 70, 96, and 80.

   a. Complete the tally sheet and frequency table below, and construct and label a frequency histogram for Sarah's grades using the accompanying grid.

Interval (grades)	Tally	Frequency
61-70		
71-80		
81-90		
91-100		

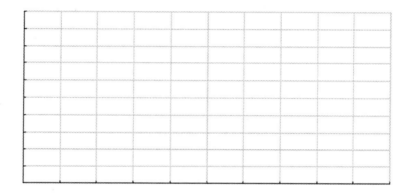

   b. Which interval contains the 75th percentile (upper quartile)?

_____

<u>June '04, #1:</u> The test scores for 10 students in Ms. Sampson's homeroom were 61, 67, 81, 83, 87, 88, 89, 90, 98, and 100. Which frequency table is accurate for this set of data?

Interval	Frequency
61-70	2
71-80	2
81-90	7
91-100	10

(1)

Interval	Frequency
61-70	2
71-80	0
81-90	8
91-100	10

(3)

Interval	Frequency
61-70	2
71-80	2
81-90	8
91-100	10

(2)

Interval	Frequency
61-70	2
71-80	0
81-90	6
91-100	2

(4)

_____

<u>Aug '04, #37:</u> The following set of data represents the scores on a mathematics quiz:

58, 79, 81, 99, 68, 92, 76, 84, 53, 57,
81, 91, 77, 50, 65, 57, 51, 72, 84, 89

Complete the frequency table below and, on the accompanying grid, draw and label a frequency histogram of these scores.

Interval	Tally	Frequency
50-59		
60-69		
70-79		
80-89		
90-99		

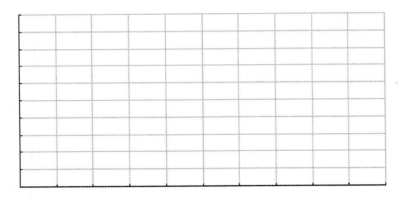

<u>Jan '05, #4:</u> The accompanying histogram shows the heights of the students in Kyra's health class.

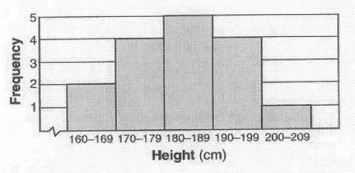

What is the total number of students in the class?

(1) 5   (2) 15   (3) 16   (4) 209

Jun '09, #38: The Fahrenheit temperature readings on 30 April mornings in Stormville, New York. are shown below:

$$41°, 58°, 61°, 54°, 49°, 46°, 52°, 58°, 67°, 43°, 47°, 60°, 52°, 58°, 48°,$$
$$44°, 59°, 66°, 62°, 55°, 44°, 49°, 62°, 61°, 59°, 54°, 57°, 58°, 63°, 60°$$

Using the data, complete the frequency table below.

Interval	Tally	Frequency
40–44		
45–49		
50–54		
55–59		
60–64		
65–69		

On the grid below, construct and label a frequency histogram based on the table.

Aug '08, #38: Twenty students were surveyed about the number of days they played outside in one week. The results of this survey are shown below.

$$\{6,5,4,3,0,7,1,5,4,4,3,2,2,3,2,4,3,4,0,7\}$$

Complete the frequency table below for these data.

Number of Days Outside

Interval	Tally	Frequency
0–1		
2–3		
4–5		
6–7		

Complete the cumulative frequency table below using these data.

Number of Days Outside

Interval	Cumulative Frequency
0–1	
0–3	
0–5	
0–7	

On the grid below, create a cumulative frequency histogram based on the table you made.

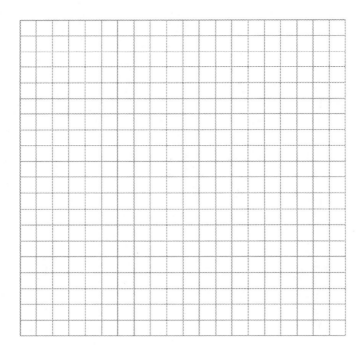

<u>Jun '08, #22</u>: The table below shows a cumulative frequency distribution of runners' ages.

**Cumulative Frequency Distribution
of Runners' Ages**

Age Group	Total
20–29	8
20–39	18
20–49	25
20–59	31
20–69	35

According to the table, how many runners are in their forties?

(1) 25   (2) 10   (3) 7   (4) 6

<u>Jun '10, #38</u>: The diagram below shows a cumulative frequency histogram of the students' test scores in Ms. Wedow's algebra class.

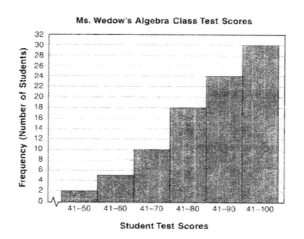

Ms. Wedow's Algebra Class Test Scores

Determine the total number of students in the class.

Determine how many students scored higher than 70 .

State which ten-point interval contains the median.

State which ten-point intervals contain the same frequency.

Circle Graphs & Bar Graphs

A bar graph is _____

_____

A circle graph (or _____) is _____

_____

_____

While you may not be asked to make either of these charts on an exam, it is important to understand them, and know what makes them different from other graphs.

The TI-73 will make both of these types of graphs as statistics plots.

To get some data for this lesson do a quick poll of the students in the room and tally the results:
(If you are doing this on your own, do a survey of the first 15 people you see.)

Which of the following colors do you prefer?

Green	_____
Blue	_____
Purple	_____
Red	_____
Pink	_____
None of the Above	_____

Read through the following example before entering your data.

In Mr. Jones' class the results of the poll were:

Green:	5
Blue:	8
Purple:	3
Red:	3
Pink:	4
Other (or no preference):	2

Total # of students = _____

The first screen shows the tally values in List 1 and the choices in List 2.

The next screen shows a circle plot with the numbers listed at the side.

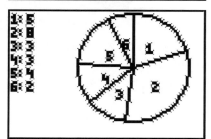

Now the numbers have been converted to a percent of the total number of people surveyed. Notice the percent symbol in the upper right corner.

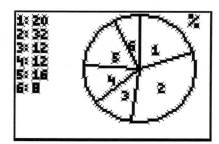

This is a bar graph displaying the same data:

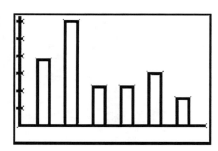

What is missing from the plots? _____

Why did we even make a category list? The screen below shows the bar graph after

TRACE has been pressed.

What is different about this screen compared to the first bar graph?

_____

_____

_____

_____

Now let's create these plots with your data.

1. Begin by entering the data (the number of people who chose each color) in L1.

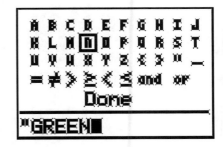

2. Go to L2. Enter the color names. ***In order for the calculator to accept the entries as category labels you must put a quotation mark at the beginning of the first entry. See the screen at the right.

3. Press done to return to the list. You should notice that a small "c" has appeared at the top of L2.

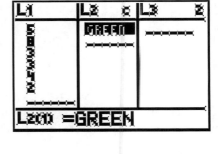

4. Finish entering the color choices in L2. Be sure that the category list is the same length as the data list.

5. Set up your plot by pressing [2ND] [Y=]. Turn the plot ON.

6. Choose the circle plot after Type. Note that when it is selected it will no longer appear to be a circle.

7. Be sure that Number is highlighted on the bottom.

8. Press [GRAPH].

9. Sketch your screen in the box below.

10. Go back and change the plot so that it will read Percent and resketch your screen.

```
┌─────────────────────────┐
│                         │
│                         │
│                         │
│                         │
│                         │
│                         │
│                         │
└─────────────────────────┘
```

11. Press [TRACE] and go around the circle. Add the colors and percents to your sketch above.

12. Change the Plot Type to Bar graph and press [GRAPH].

13. Sketch the new plot below. Be sure to use trace to add the appropriate labels to the bars.

```
┌──────────────────┐
│                  │
│                  │
│                  │
│                  │
│                  │
└──────────────────┘
```

```
┌────────────────────────────┐
│ Plot1  ▓▓ Off               │
│ Type: ▱ ▱ ▓ ▥              │
│        ⊙  ▥  ▥  ▥           │
│ CategList:L₂               │
│ DataList1:L₁               │
│ DataList2:L₃               │
│ DataList3:L₄               │
│ ▓▓▓ Hor    ▮ 2 3          │
└────────────────────────────┘
```

14. Change the setting on the plot from "Vert" to "Hor". What happens to the graph of the plot?

_____

_____

15. Name two distinct differences between the bar graphs made in this lesson and the histograms made in previous lessons.

a. _____

_____

b. _____

_____

Now we will look at two methods of reproducing our circle graphs.

First:

If we are drawing the circle by hand we will need some tools to do this neatly: a compass, a protractor, and a straightedge.

1. Use the compass to neatly make a circle in the space below.

2. Mark the center of the circle and use the straightedge to draw a radius from the center straight up to the top of the circle.

3. Enter the percents you found in #10 on the previous page in L₁.

4. How many degrees are in a complete circle? _____ Then the percents listed can be used to find the size of the angle for each section.

5. Go to the top of L2 and enter the formula L₁%360. This should create a list of the angle measurements you will need to complete your circle graph.

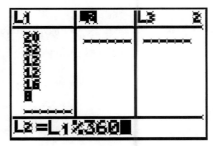

6. Use your protractor to work clockwise around your circle to make the sections of the circle the correct size.

7. Label.

Second:

You may not have an opportunity to complete this part of the lesson, but read through the directions and keep them for future use.

You can use any screen you create on your calculator in a word processing document. To save a "screen shot":

1. Have the screen exactly as you want it.

2. Have TI-Connect installed on the computer you wish to use. This comes on the CD that comes with most TI calculators or can be downloaded from education.ti.com free.

3. Connect your calculator with the computer. Many calculators come with a cable to do this but you may need to purchase one for the TI-73. They are relatively inexpensive and will have a CD with TI-Connect with them.

4. Open TI-Connect.

5. Choose TI Screen Capture.

6. It will find your device and bring up what is currently on your screen.

7. If you wish to have a border around your screen, choose .

8. Copy the picture (copy is the third icon from the left just above the screen shot).

9. Now it is available from the clipboard in a word processing document and can be used like any other picture.

Now you can insert your circle graph (or any other graph you can make on the calculator) as part of a paper to turn in!

Regents Connection

Circle Graphs
And
Bar Graphs

<u>Aug '99, #24:</u> In a recent poll, 600 people were asked whether they liked Chinese Food. A circle graph was constructed to show the results. The central angles for two of the three sectors are shown in the accompanying diagram. How many people had no opinion?

<u>June '04, #22:</u> The accompanying circle graph shows how the Marino family spends its income each month.

What is the measure, in degrees of the central angle that represents the percentage of income spent on food?

(1) 25   (2) 50   (3) 90   (4) 360

<u>Aug '04, #35:</u> The accompanying circle graph shows the favorite colors of the 300 students in the ninth grade. How many students chose red as their favorite color?

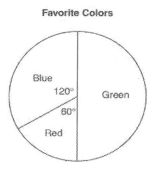

_____

<u>June '05, #38:</u> In a class of 24 students, 10 have brown hair, 8 have black hair, 4 have blonde hair, and 2 have red hair. On the accompanying diagram, construct a circle graph to show the students' hair color.

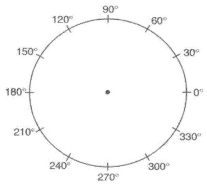

<u>Aug '05, #34:</u> Nine hundred students were asked whether they thought their school should have a dress code. A circle graph was constructed to show the results. The central angles for two of the three sectors are shown in the accompanying diagram. What is the number of students who felt that the school should have no dress code?

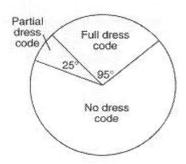

_____

<u>Jan '06, #11:</u> The accompanying circle graph shows how Shannon earned $600 during her summer vacation.

What is the measure of the central angle of the section labeled "Chores"?

(1) 30°   (2) 60°   (3) 90°   (4) 120°

A restaurant owner wanted to determine what her customers consider the most appealing quality of her restaurant. A brief survey card was placed on each table before customers were seated. A portion of the customers voluntarily completed the survey card. As an incentive, those who completed the survey card were entered in a random drawing for a new skateboard. The chart below displays the ages of those who completed the survey card:

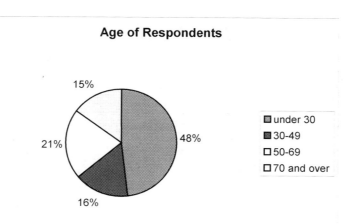

Age of Respondents

- under 30
- 30-49
- 50-69
- 70 and over

What biases might exist as a result of the design of this survey?

_____

The results of the survey are summarized in the chart below:

Best quality of the restaurant

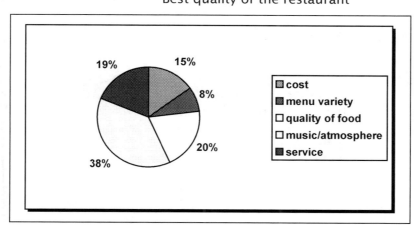

- cost
- menu variety
- quality of food
- music/atmosphere
- service

What conclusions might the restaurant owner draw from this survey?

What biases might exist in this data?

Do you believe the results of this survey are valid?

Explain your answer.

*Living Environment Aug '07, #51 – 54:

Tooth decay occurs when bacteria living in the mouth produce an acid that dissolves tooth enamel (the outer, protective covering of a tooth).

The Effect of Sugar Intake on Tooth Decay

World Regions	Average Sugar Intake per Person (kg/year)	Average Number of Teeth with Decay per Person
Americas	40	3.0
Africa	18	1.7
Southeast Asia	14	1.6
Europe	36	2.6

Using the information in the data table, construct a bar graph on the grid provided on the next page, following the directions below.

Mark an appropriate scale on the axis labeled "Average Sugar Intake per Person".

Construct vertical bars in the bracketed area for each world region to represent the "Average Sugar Intake per Person." Place the bars on the left side of each bracketed region and shade the bars as shown below. (The bar for Americas has been done for you.)

Construct vertical bars in the bracketed area for each world region to represent the "Average Number of Teeth with Decay per Person." Place the bars on the right side of each bracketed region and shade in each bar as shown below.

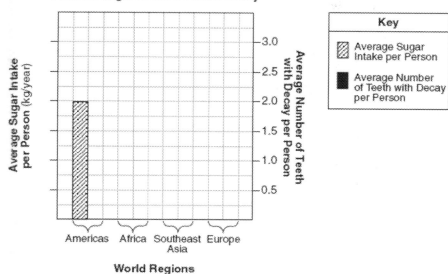

Effect of Sugar Intake on Tooth Decay

Average Sugar Intake per Person (kg/year)

Average Number of Teeth with Decay per Person

Key

Average Sugar Intake per Person

Average Number of Teeth with Decay per Person

Americas Africa Southeast Asia Europe

World Regions

Which statement is a valid conclusion regarding tooth decay?

(1) As sugar intake increases, the acidity in the mouth decreases, reducing tooth decay.

(2) As sugar intake increases, tooth decay increases in Europe and the Americas, but not in Africa and Southeast Asia.

(3) The greater the sugar intake, the greater the average number of decayed teeth.

(4) The greater the sugar intake, the faster a tooth decays.

Scatter Plots

A scatter plot is _____
_____
_____

Like most of our plots (graphs) the horizontal axis will represent the _____
_____ and the vertical axis will represent the
_____ .

We can create scatter plots on the TI-73:

1. Enter the data for the independent variable in L1.

2. Enter the data for the dependent variable in L2.

3. Press [2ND] [Y=] .

4. Turn Plot 1 ON.

5. Choose the scatter plot – the first choice in the Types.

6. Check to be sure the list that your independent variable is entered in is listed as the Xlist and the list that your dependent variable is entered in is listed as the Ylist.

7. Press [ZOOM] and choose 7:ZoomStat.

```
Plot1 On Off
Type: ▰ ⩘ ⨯⨯ ▥
       ⊕ ▦ ▨ ▥
Xlist:L1
Ylist:L2▮
Mark: □ * ×
```

Although this will give you what the calculator has determined to be a good view of the data, you may need to adjust the window to more "normal" settings.

The table below gives the average temperature each month for Lowville, NY.

Jan	Feb	Mar	Apr	May	Jun	Jul	Aug	Sep	Oct	Nov	Dec
16.6	19.1	30	42.8	54.6	63.3	67.9	65.8	57.8	47.4	36.5	22.7

Source: www.weatherbase.com

Using the number of the month, enter the months in L1 and the temperatures in L2. Create a scatter plot on your calculator following the steps above. Change the window so that it matches the one below, then sketch your screen in the space provided.

```
WINDOW
 Xmin=0
 Xmax=12
 ΔX=.1276595744...
 Xscl=1
 Ymin=0
 Ymax=80
 Yscl=4
```

The next challenge is to transfer this plot **nicely** to a grid.

The grid below is 20 x 20. The y-scale in your window was chosen so that the tick marks on your screen would match those on the grid. How was it determined that the y-scale should be 4?

_____

_____

Since you will need to fit more than 10, but less than 20 on the x-axis, it is probably best to leave the x-scale as 1.

Note that pressing [TRACE] will show you the exact coordinates of each point. This may help you to plot the points more quickly and accurately. Be sure to include all of the appropriate labels and a title for your graph!

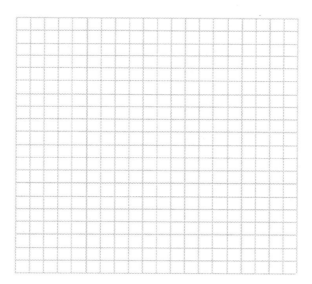

Practice:

Use the data below to create a scatter plot on your TI-73, sketch your screen, then transfer the scatter plot to the grid provided.

Lowest Recorded Temperature

Jan	Feb	Mar	Apr	May	Jun	Jul	Aug	Sep	Oct	Nov	Dec
-35	-36	-25	-4	20	28	37	29	22	9	-15	-40

***Be sure to indicate window dimensions on your sketch!

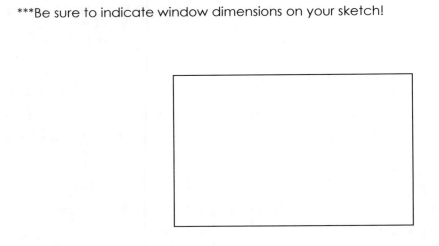

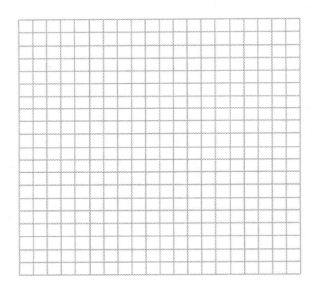

Scatter Plots

A.CM.1g, A.S.7a

A student surveyed ten of his friends on how much time they spent studying for a recent math test and their grade on the test.

Time Spent Studying vs. Test Grade

Time Spent Studying (hours)	Grade
6	100
5	98
5.25	97
4	90
4.5	87
3	85
3.75	83
4	80
2	75
1	66

Create a scatter plot of this information.

Given the following data of the weights (lbs) of 10 different cars and their respective gas mileages (mpg):

Weight (lbs)	2100	2200	2200	2800	2850	3000	3000	3500	3600	5000
Gas Mileage (mpg)	36	37	33	39	37	32	29	28	18	16

Construct a scatter plot

Jan '05, #15: Which scatter diagram shows the strongest positive correlation?

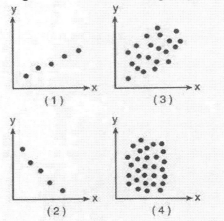

<u>Jan '10, #19</u>: Which scatter plot shows the relationship between x and y if x represents a student score on a test and y represents the number of incorrect answers a student received on the same test?

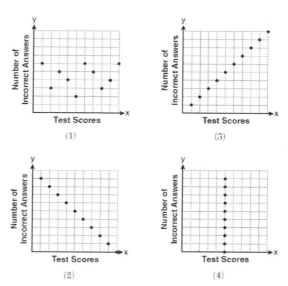

Number of Incorrect Answers

Test Scores

(1)   (3)

(2)   (4)

<u>Sample #1</u>: For 10 days, Romero kept a record of the number of hours he spent listening to music. The information is shown in the table below.

Day	1	2	3	4	5	6	7	8	9	10
Hours	9	3	2	6	8	6	10	4	5	2

Which scatter plot shows Romero's data graphically?

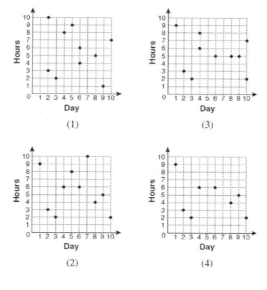

(1)   (3)

(2)   (4)

GCF & LCM

You should be familiar with "GCF" and "LCM".

Recall that GCF stands for _____ and

the GCF is _____

_____

_____

LCM stands for _____ and the LCM

is _____

_____

_____

GCF is useful for _____

_____

LCM is useful for _____

_____

The TI-73 will find these for us – with a slight twist. Instead of GCF, the TI-73 calls it the

_____ . Recall that a factor is _____

_____

_____ .

They are calling the factor a _____ instead.

***It will also only do two at a time!! If you wish to find the LCM or GCD of three or more

numbers, do the first two numbers, then use the answer with the third, and so on.

To find the GCF (GCD):

1. Press **MATH** .

2. Choose 2:gcd(

3. Enter the two numbers, separated by a comma.

4. Close the parentheses and press **ENTER** .

```
gcd(24,52)█
```

Try it now:

Find the GCF of 24 and 52.

_____

To find the LCM:

1. Press **MATH** .
2. Choose 1:lcm(
3. Enter the two numbers, separated by a comma.
4. Close the parentheses and press **ENTER** .

Try it now:

Find the LCM of 12 and 15.

```
lcm(12,15)█
```

_____

Find the LCM of 9, 24, and 5. (Remember – this must be done in two steps!!)

```
lcm(9,24)       72
lcm(72,5)█
```

_____

Practice:

Find the GCF:

1. 14, 49

    _____

2. 51, 39

    _____

3. 120, 200

    _____

4. 55, 100

    _____

5. 200. 150, 120

    _____

6. 130, 39, 52

    _____

7. 240, 300, 1200

    _____

8. $63,74,85$

9. Factor $26x - 104x^2$

10. Factor $108p^3 - 27p^2 + 54p$

Find the LCM:

11. $4,30$

12. $10,35$

13. 34.54

14. $27,90,108$

15. $33,54,81$

16. Find the least common denominator: $\dfrac{5}{27}, \dfrac{8}{108}$

17. Find the least common denominator: $\dfrac{1}{12}, \dfrac{4}{13}, \dfrac{5}{52}$

18. Find the least common denominator: $\dfrac{20}{21}, \dfrac{5}{14}, \dfrac{6}{37}$

Manual Line
Of
Best Fit

From a scatter plot, we can use the points to help us to find an equation of a line that will help us use the data to predict results for other inputs.

This is called the _____ .

On paper we can use a straight edge to help determine the line. On the TI-73 we can use

_____ .

Let's start on paper.

1. Create a scatter plot using the following data:

x	2	4	6	8	10
y	18	15	12	10	8

2. Use a straightedge to draw a line that comes close to hitting all of the data points.

3. Choose two points that lie exactly on the line – they do not need to be points in the original data table but they can be:

   _____   _____

4. Find the slope of the line using the formula $m = \dfrac{\Delta y}{\Delta x} = \dfrac{y_2 - y_1}{x_2 - x_1}$.

   _____

5. Use the formula $y - y_1 = m(x - x_1)$ to find the equation of the line through the two points.

Now let's find it on the TI-73:

1. Create a scatter plot on your screen. Use the window given below and sketch your screen in the space provided.

2. While you are at the graphing screen, press 2ND LIST

3. Arrow over to CALC and choose 3:Manual-Fit.

4. You should be back at the graphing screen. Use the arrows to move the cursor to a point that appears to be on the line of best fit. Press ENTER .

5. Now as you move the cursor a line should appear. Align this with the points on the screen until it looks "close" to the points on the scatter plot.

6. Press ENTER .

7. The equation of the line you have placed on the screen should appear across the top of the screen now.

Although this may not match exactly the equation that you found using formulas, it should be relatively close.
**A manual line of best fit is not meant to be exact!!

Using our formula we can predict what would happen at points not included in the data list.

Suppose we want to predict what would happen when $x = 5$? Solve for y when x is 5.

_____

Because the number 5 is within the range of the original x-values, this is called

_____ .

Suppose we want to predict what would happen when $x = 20$? Solve for y when x is 20.

_____

Because the number 20 is beyond the range of the original x-values, this is called

_____ .

Practice:
For each set of data
      a. Create a scatter plot.
      b. Use Manual-Fit to find the equation of the line of best fit.
      c. Sketch your screen showing the points on the scatter plot and the line you have found. Be sure to indicate your window dimensions!
      d. Use the equation to predict what would happen at $x = 10$ and at $x = 100$.

1. Equation: _____

x	4	8	12	16	20
y	25	18	14	9	5

      Prediction: $x = 10$ _____

                   $x = 100$ _____

2. Equation: _____

x	6	12	18	21	25
y	2	10	20	28	36

Prediction: $x = 10$ _____

                   $x = 100$ _____

3. Equation: _____

x	1	7	15	20	30
y	40	33	25	19	10

Prediction: $x = 10$ _____

                   $x = 100$ _____

Regents Connection

Line of Best Fit

Aug '09, #30: The number of hours spent on math homework each week and the final exam grades for twelve students in Mr. Dylan's algebra class are plotted below.

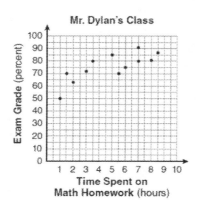

Based on a line of best fit, which exam grade is the best prediction for a student who spends about 4 hours on math homework each week?

(1) 62   (2) 72   (3) 82   (4) 92

_____

Jun '09, #36: The table below shows the number of prom tickets sold over a ten-day period.

Prom Ticket Sales

Day (x)	1	2	5	7	10
Number of Prom Tickets Sold (y)	30	35	55	60	70

Plot these data points on the coordinate grid below. Use a consistent and appropriate scale. Draw a reasonable line of best fit and write its equation.

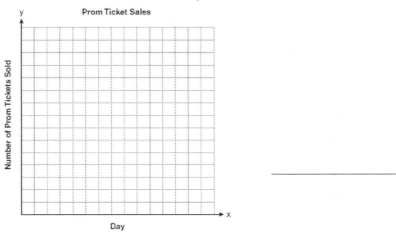

<u>Aug '08, #22</u>: Which equation most closely represents the line of best fit for the scatter plot below?

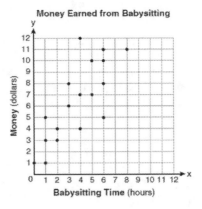

Money Earned from Babysitting

(1) $y = x$

(3) $y = \dfrac{3}{2}x + 4$

(2) $y = \dfrac{2}{3}x + 1$

(4) $y = \dfrac{3}{2}x + 1$

<u>Jun '10, #36</u>: Megan and Bryce opened a new store called the Donut Pit. Their goal is to reach a profit of $20,000 in their 18*th* month of business. The table and scatter plot below represent the profit, P, in thousands of dollars, that they made during the first 12 months.

t (months)	1	2	3	4	5	6	7	8	9	10	11	12
P (profit, in thousands of dollars)	3.0	2.5	4.0	5.0	6.5	5.5	7.0	6.0	7.5	7.0	9.0	9.5

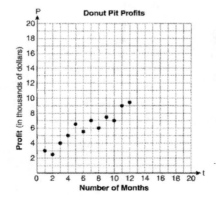

Donut Pit Profits

Draw a reasonable line of best fit.

Using the line of best fit, predict whether Megan and Bryce will reach their goal in the 18*th* month of their business. Justify your answer.

_____

_____

Linear Regression

The word *regression* was first used by Sir Francis Galton (1822-1911) in the late 19th century.

A study by Galton revealed that the heights of the children of tall parents were above average, but seemed to fall back, *or regress,* toward the mean (average) height of the population.

Thus, the general process of predicting one variable (such as a child's height) based on another variable (the parent's heights) became known as regression.

The TI-73 will do many types of regression:

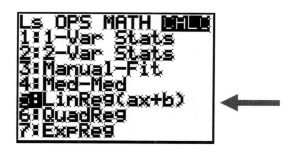

The most used type of regression for our purposes will be 5:LinReg(ax+b). This is a

_____ _____and may be used to approximate the

_____ if the question does not specify that it must be done manually, as in the previous lesson.

The previous menu can be found by pressing [2ND] [LIST] and using the arrow key to move the cursor to CALC.

The linear regression requires that you fill two lists with data and that the lists be of <u>equal length</u>. The data should be matched in the lists and there should be two or more items in each list.

The first list should contain the _____variable. (x)

The second list should contain the _____variable. (y)

Think of it as: _____

_____

Or, in the case above, the parent's height was the independent variable. The children studied were chosen because their parents were tall, but did the child's height depend on the parent's height?

Notes:

1. "a" is the _____ (what we usually call _____)

2. "b" is the _____

3. If the question does not specifically state the appropriate place to round to, there are two possible ways to correctly write the answer.

   a. Write all of the digits visible on your screen!

      or

   b. Convert "a" and "b" to fractions. This is more calculator work but usually results in less written work – you choose. The directions are given in Appendix D if you choose to convert to fractions.

Example:

A. Starting really simple: find the equation of the line that passes through the points (6,-3) and (5,7).

1. Enter the x's in List 1.

2. Enter the y's in List 2 (in the same order the x's were entered.)

3. Press [2ND] [LIST] .

4. Move over to Calc

5. Choose 5:LinReg

6. If L1 and L2 are your only lists and they are in the correct order, press [ENTER] .

7. If you have other lists or need to change the order, enter the list names with a comma between them then press [ENTER] .

8. Write the equation with the given values of a, _____ , and b, _____ , in their correct places.

The equation of the line through the given points is

_____ .

***Note that if the question only requires you to find the slope or y-intercept, this method works for those questions also!!

Practice:

Using the LinReg (linear regression) command, find the equations of the lines through the following pairs of points and sketch the graph of the line. Remember that sketches must be properly labeled for full credit!!

To match the axes provided, be sure that you have done a Zoom Standard followed by a Zoom Square.

1. $(1,5)$, $(3,6)$

a=_____

b=_____

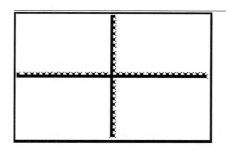

2. $(0,5)$, $(-4,8)$

a=_____

b=_____

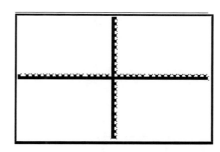

3. $(0,4)$, $(-1,-1)$

a=_____

b=_____

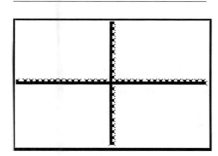

4. $(2,3)$, $(0,7)$

a=_____

b=_____

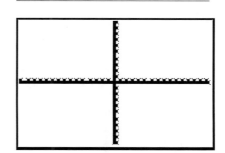

5. $(0,0)$, $(9,8)$

a=_____

b=_____

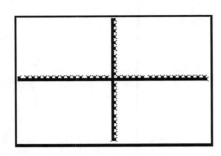

6. $(-1,0)$, $(3,-4)$

a=_____

b=_____

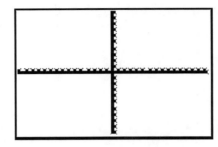

7. $(6,8)$, $(-4,-4)$

a=_____

b=_____

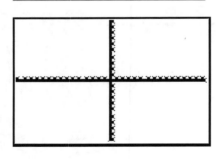

8. $(4,2)$, $(0,-10)$

a=_____

b=_____

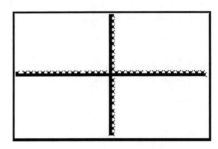

9. $(3,3)$, $(2,2)$

a=_____

b=_____

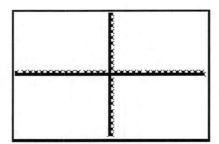

10. $(1,9)$, $(1,7)$

***See next page.

a=_____

b=_____

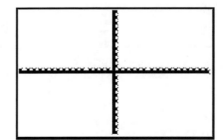

11. $(1,4)$, $(5,4)$

     a=_____

     b=_____

_____

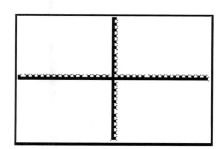

12. $(2,7)$, $(2,18)$

     a=_____

     b=_____

_____

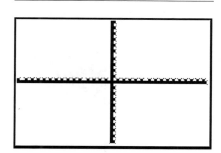

You should take note of some things that happened.

What happened when you attempted to do a linear regression on #10?

_____

_____

_____

Graph the points given in #10 below and draw the line that passes through the two points.

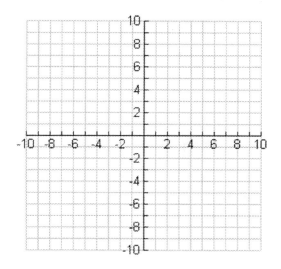

What type of line did you graph? _____

What is the slope of the line that passes through the two points? _____

So we were asking the graphing calculator to find something that does not exist!! This is why the screen below appeared.

```
ERR:DOMAIN
1 Quit
2 Goto
```

How do we write the equation of a vertical line? _____
_____

So when you see that _____
you can write the equation of the line by _____
_____

Now you should be able to complete #10 (and one other question) without further assistance fromthTI-73.

How was #11 different? _____
_____

Be sure that you use the **simplest form** of the equation of the line. If $a = 0$, do not write the first term. Likewise, if $b = 0$, do not write $+0$ at the end of the equation.

Correlation

When we do a linear regression we also want to know how well the data "fits" the line.

To do this we must activate the _____

Go to the CATALOG ([2ND] [PRGM]).

Find DiagnosticOn.

```
CATALOG
 DependAsk
 DependAuto
 DiagnosticOff
▶DiagnosticOn
 dice(
 dim(
 Disp
```

Press [ENTER] two times.

This is one of the few functions of the calculator that can be accessed only in the catalog! The diagnostic will stay on until you turn it off (which you never NEED to do) or the calculator is reset.
This will give us an "r" value that will tell us how well our data fits the equation found.

r-values

If all the data points lie exactly on the line and the slope of the line is

_____ (the line goes "uphill"), the correlation coefficient, r, is_____.
We say that the data in the lists have a _____

_____ .

Similarly, if the data points are all exactly on the line and the slope of the line is

_____(the line goes "downhill"), the correlation coefficient is

_____. Now the data have a _____

_____ .

If, when you make your scatter plot, the points don't seem to make a line at all you will find

that _____. In other words, if r is close to zero when you calculate the

regression on the graphing calculator, it is not a "good fit" and there is little or no

_____ .

Guidelines:

How close it needs to be will depend on the type of data we are using:

1. If the data is from a scientific experiment we would like to see
$$0.9 \leq r \leq 1 \quad \text{or} \quad -1 \leq r \leq -0.9$$

2. If the data is from a social science experiment we would like to see
$$0.7 \leq r \leq 1 \quad \text{or} \quad -1 \leq r \leq -0.7$$

You will also see "r^2". We will _not_ need this value, <u>only the "r"</u>.
*****The slope and r should always have the same sign!!!

Example:
The boiling point of water is a function of altitude. The table shows the boiling points at different altitudes.

Location	Altitude h meters	Boiling Point of water t°C
Halifax, NS	0	100
Banff, Alberta	1383	95
Quito, Ecuador	2850	90
Mt. Logan	5951	80

a. Find the regression equation for the function.

_____

b. Give the "r" value for this equation.

_____

c. Is r closer to 1, -1, or 0? What does this mean about the correlation of the data?

_____

_____

_____

Practice:

For each set of ordered pairs:
   a. Approximate the equation of the line of best fit by calculating the linear regression. Coefficients may be rounded to the nearest hundredth.
   b. Give the r-value for each regression.
   c. Discuss the correlation between the x and y values.
   d. Create a scatter plot of the data on the graphing calculator. Use a Standard Window.
   e. Graph the equation found on the graphing calculator.
   f. Sketch the screen showing both the scatter plot and the line.

1. $(-2,-7),(0,-1),(4,5),(6,7),(8,10)$

    a. _____

    b. _____

    c. _____

    _____

    d. - f.

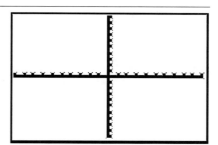

2. $(-2,8),(-1,6),(2,3),(6,-1),(9,-5)$

    a. _____

    b. _____

    c. _____

    _____

    d. - f.

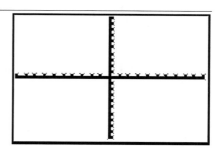

3. $(-8,3),(-5,0),(-1,1),(2,0),(4,-1)$

    a. _____

    b. _____

    c. _____

    _____

    d. - f.

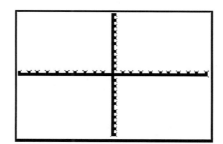

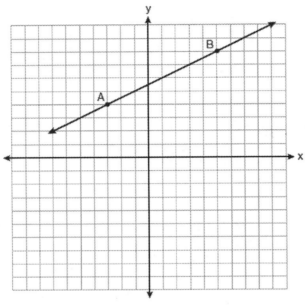

Regents Connection

Lines

Jan '10, #7: In the diagram below, what is the slope of the line passing through points A and B?

(1) -2 (2) 2 (3) $-\dfrac{1}{2}$ (4) $\dfrac{1}{2}$

_____

Jan '10, #13: Which equation represents the line that passes through the points $(-3,7)$ and $(3,3)$?

(1) $y = \dfrac{2}{3}x + 1$ (3) $y = -\dfrac{2}{3}x + 5$

(2) $y = \dfrac{2}{3}x + 9$ (4) $-\dfrac{2}{3}x + 9$

_____

Jan '10, #21: Which point is on the line $4y - 2x = 0$?

(1) $(-2,-1)$ (2) $(-2,1)$ (3) $(-1,-2)$ (4) $(1,2)$

_____

Jan '10, #26: Which equation represents a line parallel to the graph of $2x - 4y = 16$?

(1) $y = \dfrac{1}{2}x - 5$ (3) $y = -2x + 6$

(2) $y = -\dfrac{1}{2}x + 4$ (4) $y = 2x + 8$

_____

Aug '09, #11: Which equation represents a line parallel to the x-axis?

(1) $y = -5$ (2) $y = -5x$ (3) $x = 3$ (4) $x = 3y$

_____

Aug '09, #15: What is the slope of the line that passes through the points $(-5, 4)$ and $(15, -4)$?

(1) $-\dfrac{2}{5}$ (2) 0 (3) $-\dfrac{5}{2}$ (4) undefined

_____

Aug '09, #27: What is an equation of the line that passes through the point $(3, -1)$ and has a slope of 2?

(1) $y = 2x + 5$ (3) $y = 2x - 4$

(2) $y = 2x - 1$ (4) $y = 2x - 7$

_____

Jun '09, #22: What is an equation of the line that passes through the point $(4, -6)$ and has a slope of -3?

(1) $y = -3x + 6$ (3) $y = -3x + 10$

(2) $y = -3x - 6$ (4) $y = -3x + 14$

_____

Jan '09, #10: What is an equation of the line that passes through the points $(3, -3)$ and $(-3, -3)$?

(1) $y = 3$ (2) $x = -3$ (3) $y = -3$ (4) $x = y$

_____

<u>Jan '09, #13</u>: What is the slope of the line that passes through the points $(2,5)$ and $(7,3)$?

(1) $-\dfrac{5}{2}$ (2) $-\dfrac{2}{5}$ (3) $\dfrac{8}{9}$ (4) $\dfrac{9}{8}$

_____

<u>Jan '09, #26</u>: Which equation represents a line that is parallel to the line $y = 3 - 2x$?

(1) $4x + 2y = 5$ (3) $y = 3 - 4x$
(2) $2x + 4y = 1$ (4) $y = 4x - 2$

_____

<u>Jan '09, #33</u>: The table below represents the number of hours a student worked and the amount of money the student earned.

Number of Hours (h)	Dollars Earned (d)
8	$50.00
15	$93.75
19	$118.75
30	$187.50

Write an equation that represents the number of dollars, d, earned in terms of the number of hours, h, worked.

_____

Using this equation, determine the number of dollars the student would earn for working 40 hours.

_____

<u>Aug '08, #10</u>: Which equation represents a line parallel to the x-axis?

(1) $x = 5$ (2) $y = 10$ (3) $x = \dfrac{1}{3}y$ (4) $y = 5x + 17$

_____

<u>Aug '08, #23</u>: In a linear equation, the independent variable increases at a constant rate while the dependent variable decreases at a constant rate. The slope of this line s

(1) zero   (2) negative   (3) positive   (4) undefined

_____

<u>Aug '08, #36</u>: Write an equation that represents the line that passes through the points $(5,4)$ and $(-5,0)$.

<u>Jun '08, #1</u>: Which graph represents a linear function?

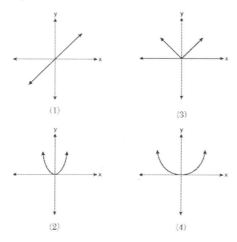

(1)

(3)

(2)

(4)

<u>Jun '08, #14</u>: Which equation represents a line that is parallel to the line $y = -4x + 5$?

(1) $y = -4x + 3$

(3) $y = \dfrac{1}{4}x + 3$

(2) $y = -\dfrac{1}{4}x + 5$

(4) $y = 4x + 5$

<u>Jun '08, #20</u>: What is the slope of the line that passes through the points $(-6,1)$ and $(4,-4)$?

(1) -2 (2) 2 (3) $-\dfrac{1}{2}$ (4) $\dfrac{1}{2}$

<u>Aug '00, #9:</u> Which equation represents a line parallel to the line $y = 2x - 5$?

(1 $y = 2x + 5$

(3) $y = 5x - 2$

(2) $y = -\dfrac{1}{2}x - 5$

(4) $y = -2x - 5$

Integrated Algebra on the TI-73

<u>June '99, #18:</u> What is the slope of line l shown in the accompanying diagram?

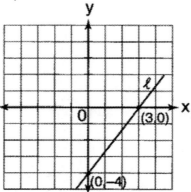

(1) $\dfrac{4}{3}$ (2) $\dfrac{3}{4}$ (3) $-\dfrac{3}{4}$ (4) $-\dfrac{4}{3}$

<u>Aug '01, #30:</u> Shanaya graphed the line represented by the equation $y = x - 6$. Write an equation for a line that is parallel to the given line.

Write an equation for a line that is perpendicular to the given line.

Write an equation for a line that is identical to the given line but has different coefficients.

<u>June '02, #5:</u> What is the slope of the linear equation $5y - 10x = -15$?

(1) 10 (2) 2 (3) –10 (4) –15

<u>Jan '02, #3:</u> What is the slope of the line whose equation is $2y = 5x + 4$?

(1) 5 (2) 2 (3) $\dfrac{5}{2}$ (4) $\dfrac{2}{5}$

<u>Jan '00, #24</u>: A straight line with slope 5 contains the points $(1,2)$ and $(3,k)$. Find the value of k. [The use of the accompanying grid is optional.]

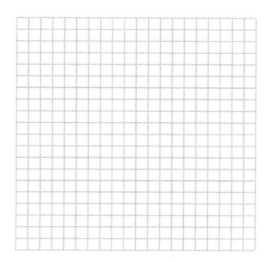

<u>Sample #13</u>: What is an equation for the line that passes through the coordinates $(2,0)$ and $(0,3)$?

(1) $y = -\dfrac{3}{2}x + 3$ (3) $y = -\dfrac{2}{3}x + 2$

(2) $y = -\dfrac{3}{2}x - 3$ (4) $y = -\dfrac{2}{3}x - 2$

<u>Sample #16</u>: What is the slope of the line containing the points $(3,4)$ and $(-6,10)$?

(1) $\dfrac{1}{2}$ (2) 2 (3) $-\dfrac{2}{3}$ (4) $-\dfrac{3}{2}$

<u>Jun '10, #4</u>: What is the slope of the line that passes through the points $(3,5)$ and $(-2,2)$?

(1) $\dfrac{1}{5}$ (2) $\dfrac{3}{5}$ (3) $\dfrac{5}{3}$ (4) 5

<u>Jun '10, #7</u>: Which linear equation represents a line containing the point $(1,3)$?

(1) $x + 2y = 5$ (3) $2x + y = 5$

(2) $x - 2y = 5$ (4) $2x - y = 5$

_____

<u>Jun '10, #15</u>: The graphs of the equations $y = 2x - 7$ and $y - kx = 7$ are parallel when k equals

(1) -2 (2) 2 (3) -7 (4) 7

_____

Correlation

<u>Jan '10, #30</u>: Which situation describes a correlation that is not a causal relationship?

    (1) the length of the edge of a cube and the volume of the cube
    (2) the distance traveled and the time spent driving
    (3) the age of a child and the number of siblings the child has
    (4) the number of classes taught in a school and the number of teachers
           employed

_____

<u>Aug '09, #8</u>: Which relationship can best be described as causal?

    (1) height and intelligence
    (2) shoe size and running speed
    (3) number of correct answers on a test and test score
    (4) number of students in a class and number of students with brown hair

_____

<u>Jun '08, #5</u>: There is a negative correlation between the number of hours a student watches television and his or her social studies test score. Which scatter plot below displays this correlation?

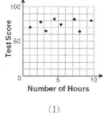

(1)

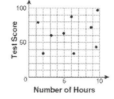

(3)

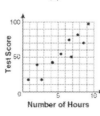

(2)

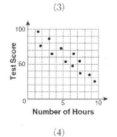

(4)

_____

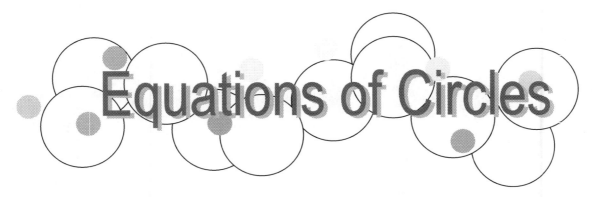

Equations of Circles

A circle in the coordinate plane can be completely described by identifying the _____ of the circle and how far out the circle reaches from that point (how far it "radiates", hence the term "_____").

The equation of a circle is important to recognize:

$$(x-x_c)^2+(y-y_c)^2=r^2$$

where (x_c, y_c) is the *center* of the circle and r is the *radius*.

There are three ways to make a circle on the TI-73:

1. The equation can be entered in the Y= menu, but it must be done in "half circles". This can be very cumbersome!

2. An easier way is to DRAW the circle.

    One way to DRAW a circle is:

    a. Begin at the home screen.

    b. Press DRAW .

    c. Choose 6:Circle(

        *** Common mistake: Do not choose 1:ClrDraw!!
        Clr stands for CLEAR not
        circle!!********************

    ```
    Circle(x,y,r)
    ```

    d. The circle command requires you to input *three* pieces of information: the x and y values for the center of the circle and the radius.

e.   Press [ENTER] . The circle should appear in the graph window.

******Do not press** [GRAPH] ! !!! If you have not pressed [ENTER] on the

home screen, your circle will not appear on the graphing screen. Remember

that you are "DRAWing" not "GRAPHing".

f.   Change the ZOOM setting to make the circle a "circle" rather than an

"oval".   (Hint: ZDecimal or Zsquare work well for this!)

g.   Note that sometimes making changes or additions to your screen will

cause your circle to "disappear". Just return to the home screen and

press [2ND] [ENTER] to "backspace" to your circle command

and press [ENTER]

3.   The third way to graph a circle also uses the DRAW command, but you will need to
begin in the graphing window.

a. Press [GRAPH] .

b. Press [DRAW]

c.   Choose 6:Circle(

d.   Use the arrows to move the flashing cursor to the point that is to be the

center of the circle.   Press [ENTER] . (The cursor might be difficult

to see at first because it is at the origin until you press the arrow keys.)

e.   Move the cursor up, down, left, or right the number of units the radius of

the circle is. Press [ENTER] .

f.   The circle should appear. **This method is less reliable because you

can't place the center exactly where you want it unless it is centered

at the origin.

When finished Clear Draw before beginning another circle. (Choice 1 on the DRAW
menu.)

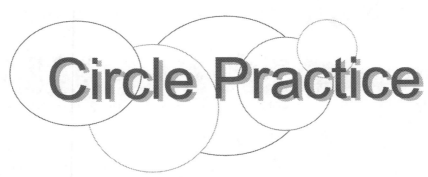

Circle Practice

Part 1. Using the given center and radius, graph the circle using the DRAW command. Sketch the circle in the box provided. Do a Zoom Standard then a Zoom Square so that your screen matches the boxes below.
***If the entire circle does not appear on the screen only sketch the part you can see.

1. $(0,0)$, $r = 4$

2. $(1,3)$, $r = 3$

3. $(-2,4)$, $r = 5$

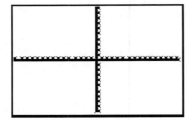 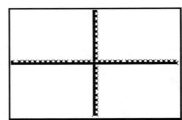 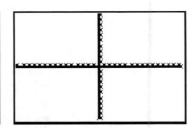

4. $(-3,-5)$, $r = 4$

5. $(0,0)$, $r = 10$

6. $(1,5)$, $r = 5$

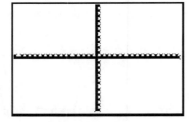 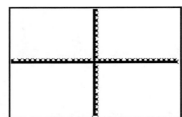 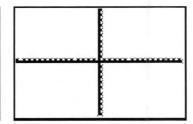

7. $(0,8)$, $r = 2$

8. $(-10,0)$, $r = 6$

9. $(0,10)$, $r = 4$

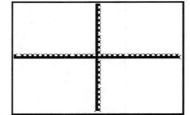 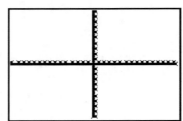 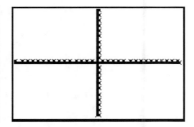

Part 2. Given the equation of a circle, identify the center and the radius; then continue as in Part 1.

Example: $(x-2)^2 + (y+3)^2 = 16$

Center = $(2,-3)$ **Note the sign change!!

Radius = $\sqrt{16} = 4$

1. $(x-1)^2 + (y-1)^2 = 25$

Center=_____

Radius=_____

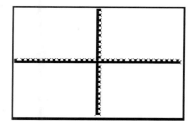

2. $(x+3)^2 + (y-2)^2 = 81$

Center=_____

Radius=_____

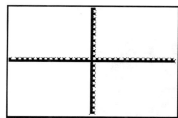

3. $(x-7)^2 + (y-1)^2 = 25$

Center=_____

Radius=_____

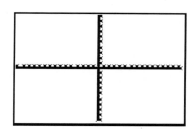

4. $(x-2)^2 + (y-5)^2 = 9$

Center=_____

Radius=_____

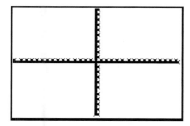

5. $(x+5)^2 + (y+5)^2 = 16$

Center=_____

Radius=_____

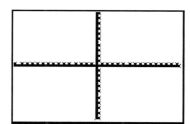

6. $(x-8)^2 + (y-7)^2 = 36$

Center=_____

Radius=_____

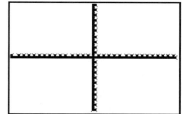

7. $x^2 + (y+5)^2 = 64$

Center=_____

Radius=_____

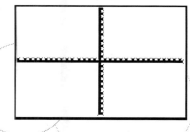

8. $(x+2)^2 + y^2 = 49$

Center=_____

Radius=_____

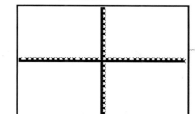

9. $x^2 + y^2 = 1$

Center=_____

Radius=_____

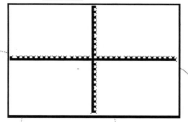

Regents Connection

Circles

June '99, #14: What is the diameter of a circle whose circumference is 5?

(1) $\dfrac{2.5}{\pi^2}$ (2) $\dfrac{2.5}{\pi}$ (3) $\dfrac{5}{\pi^2}$ (4) $\dfrac{5}{\pi}$

_____

June '99, #31: A target shown in the accompanying diagram consists of three circles with the same center. The radii of the circles have lengths of 3 inches, 7 inches, and 9 inches.

a. What is the area of the shaded region to the nearest tenth of a square inch?

_____

b. To the nearest percent, what percent of the target is shaded?

_____

Jan '00, #12: If the circumference of a circle is 10π inches, what is the area, in square inches, of the circle?

(1) 110π (2) 25π (3) 50π (4) 100π

_____

June '00, #8: Which equation represents a circle whose center is $(3,-2)$?

(1) $(x+3)^2+(y-2)^2=4$

(2) $(x-3)^2+(y+2)^2=4$

(3) $(x+2)^2+(y-3)^2=4$

(4) $(x-2)^2+(y+3)^2=4$

_____

<u>June '01, #19:</u> What is the total number of points of intersection in the graphs of the equations $x^2 + y^2 = 16$ and $y = 4$?

(1) 1   (3) 3

(2) 2   (4) 0

_____

<u>Aug '01, #5:</u> In the accompanying diagram, a circle with radius 4 is inscribed in a square.

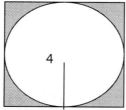

4

What is the area of the shaded region?

(1) $64 - 16\pi$ (3) $64\pi - 8\pi$

(2) $16 - 16\pi$ (4) $16 - 8\pi$

_____

<u>Aug '00, #27:</u> To measure the length of a hiking trail, a worker uses a device with a 2-foot-diameter wheel that counts the number of revolutions the wheel makes. If the device reads 1,100.5 revolutions at the end of the trail, how many miles long is the trail, to the nearest tenth of a mile.

_____

<u>Aug '01, #8:</u> What is the approximate circumference of a circle with radius 3?

(1) 7.07   (2) 9.42   (3) 18.85   (4) 28,27

_____

<u>June '02, #15:</u> If the circumference of a circle is doubled, the diameter of the circle

(1) remains the same   (3) is multiplied by 4

(2) increases by 2   (4) is doubled

_____

June '01, #29: Virginia has a circular rug on her square living room floor, as represented in the accompanying diagram. If her entire living room floor measures 100 square feet, what is the area of the part of the floor covered by the rug?

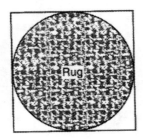

June '00, #28: Tamika has a hard rubber ball whose circumference measures 13 inches. She wants to box it for a gift but can only find cube-shaped boxes of sides 3 inches, 4 inches, 5 inches, or 6 inches. What is the smallest box that the ball will fit into with the top on?

Sample #30: Ms. Brown plans to carpet part of her living room floor. The living room floor is a square 20 feet by 20 feet. She wants to carpet a quarter-circle as shown below.

20'

Find, to the nearest square foot, what part of the floor will remain uncarpeted. Show how you arrived at your answer.

Jan '04, #26: In the coordinate plane, the points $(2,2)$ and $(2,12)$ are the endpoints of a diameter of a circle. What is the length of the radius of the circle?

(1) 5   (2) 6   (3) 7   (4) 10

<u>Jan '04, #37:</u> A wheel has a radius of 5 feet. What is the minimum number of complete revolutions that the wheel must make to roll at least 1,000 feet?

_____

<u>Aug '05, #28:</u> The graph of the equation $x^2 + y^2 = 4$ can be described as a

(1) line passing through points $(0,2)$ and $(2,0)$

(2) parabola with its vertex at $(0,2)$

(3) circle with its center at the origin and a radius of 2

(4) circle with its center at the origin and a radius of 4

_____

<u>Jan '06, #17:</u> A dog is tied with a rope to a stake in the ground. The length of the rope is 5 yards. What is the area, in square yards, in which the dog can roam?

(1) 25π (2) 10π (3) 25   (4) 20

_____

<u>Jan '06, #25:</u> Which point is on the circle whose equation is $x^2 + y^2 = 289$?

(1) $(-12,12)$ (2) $(7,-10)$ (3) $(-1,-16)$ (4) $(8,-15)$

_____

<u>June '06, #31:</u> Determine the area, in square feet, of the smallest square that can contain a circle with a radius of 8 feet.

_____

Functions

Functions are _____

_____

The notation f(x) is just another name for _____ .

Although f is the most frequently used letter for function notation, g and h are also commonly seen and almost any other letter is possible if appropriately defined.

Now, instead of saying "If $y = 3x^2 - 5$, what is y when $x = -2$", we can say

_____

Examples:

a. $f(x) = -2x + 4$, find $f(3)$

_____

b. $f(x) = x^2 - 3x + 4$, find $f(-1)$

_____

c. $f(x) = 4x - 15$, find $f(10)$

_____

Not every equation is a function. You may be asked to recognize a function from an equation or from a graph.

From an equation:

1. Look for y. If there is NO y in the equation it is the equation of

_____ . These

   are NOT functions.

2. Is y squared? When y is squared the equation has two possible y values for some values of x. These are NOT functions.
3. If y is there and it is not squared, the equation is the equation of a function.

From a graph:

1. Is there anywhere on the graph where you could draw a vertical line and cross the graphed line or curve in at least two places? If you can, it is NOT a function.

   This is called the _____

2. If you can also NOT draw a horizontal line that passes through the line or curve, the function is called a _____.

   (More about these in a later course!)

You can also think of it this way:

On the graphing calculator, the default mode is called FUNCTION mode. Can you graph the equation in Y= in only one step? If you can, it is a function.

Examples:
Which of the following are functions?

a. $y = 4x - 10$

b. $x = 15$

c. $y^2 = x + 2$

d. $y = 2x^2 - 3x + 6$

e.

f.

h.

i.

Which of the following is a 1-1 function?

k.

l.

m.

Practice:

1. $f(x) = 2x - 5$, find $f(-3)$

   _____

2. $f(x) = -2x^2 - x + 5$, find $f(4)$

   _____

3. Graph $2x^2 = y + 5$. Is it a function?

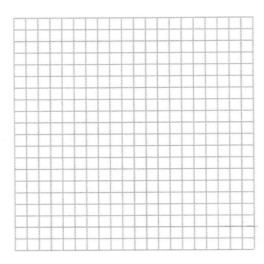

_____

4. Graph $x^2 + y^2 = 16$. Is it a function?

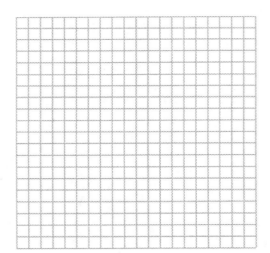

_____

5. Is every line a function? Explain.

_____

_____

6. Is the graph at the right the graph of a function?   Explain.

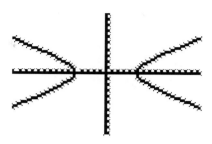

_____

7. Is the graph at the right the graph of a function?   Explain.

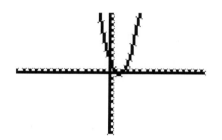

_____

8. Is the graph at the right the graph of a function? Explain.

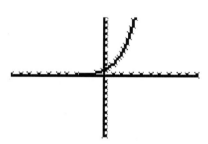

_____

9. Is the graph at the right the graph of a function? Explain.

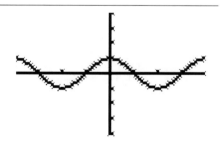

_____

Regents Connection

Functions

June '02, #16: Which diagram represents a one-to-one function?

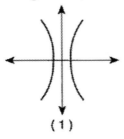
(1)

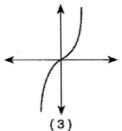
(3)

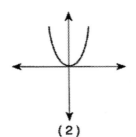
(2)

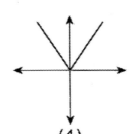
(4)

_____

Jan '02, #11: Which relation is a function?

(1) $x = 4$ (3) $y = \sin x$

(2) $x = y^2 + 1$ (4) $x^2 + y^2 = 16$

_____

Aug '01, #1: Which relation is not a function?

(1) $y = 2x + 4$ (3) $x = 3y - 2$

(2) $y = x^2 - 4x + 3$ (4) $x = y^2 + 2x - 3$

_____

June '02, #13: Which equation represents a function?

(1) $4y^2 = 36 - 9x^2$ (3) $x^2 + y^2 = 4$

(2) $y = x^2 - 3x - 4$ (4) $x = y^2 - 6x + 8$

_____

<u>June '03, #10</u>: Which diagram represents a relation in which each member of the domain corresponds to only one member of its range?

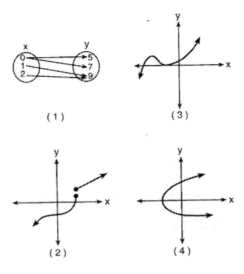

<u>Aug '03, #1</u>: Which graph does not represent a function of x?

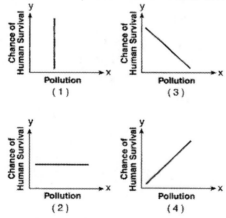

<u>June '04, #6</u>: If $f(x) = 4x^0 + (4x)^{-1}$, what is the value of $f(4)$?

(1) -12 (2) 0 (3) $1\dfrac{1}{16}$ (4) $4\dfrac{1}{16}$

<u>June '04, #7:</u> What is the domain of the function $f(x) = \dfrac{2x^2}{x^2 - 9}$?

    (1)   all real numbers except 0
    (2)   all real numbers except 3
    (3)   all real numbers except 3 and –3
    (4)   all real numbers

<u>Aug '04, #3:</u> Which set of ordered pairs is **not** a function?

    (1) $\{(3,1),\ (2,1),\ (1,2),\ (3,2)\}$

    (2) $\{(4,1),\ (5,1),\ (6,1),\ (7,1)\}$

    (3) $\{(1,2),\ (3,4),\ (4,5),\ (5,6)\}$

    (4) $\{(0,0),\ (1,1),\ (2,2),\ (3,3)\}$

<u>Jan '05, #4:</u> What is the domain of the function $f(x) = \dfrac{3x^2}{x^2 - 49}$?

    (1) $\{x \mid x \in real\ numbers, x \neq 7\}$

    (2) $\{x \mid x \in real\ numbers, x \neq \pm 7\}$

    (3) $\{x \mid x \in real\ numbers\}$

    (4) $\{x \mid x \in real\ numbers, x \neq 0\}$

<u>Jan '05, #11:</u> Which graph is *not* a function?

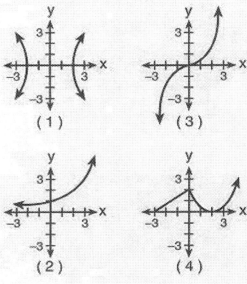

June '05, #11: Which relation is a function?

(1) $xy = 7$

(3) $x^2 - y^2 = 7$

(2) $x = 7$

(4) $x^2 + y^2 = 7$

_____

Aug '02, #4: What is the domain of $f(x) = 2^x$?

(1) all integers

(3) $x \geq 0$

(2) all real numbers

(4) $x \leq 0$

_____

Jan '10, #18: Which relation represents a function?

(1) $\{(0,3),(2,4),(0,6)\}$

(2) $\{(-7,5),(-7,1),(-10,3),(-4,3)\}$

(3) $\{(2,0),(6,2),(6,-2)\}$

(4) $\{(-6,5),(-3,2),(1,2),(6,5)\}$

_____

Aug '09, #19: Which relation is not a function?

(1) $\{(1,5),(2,6),(3,6),(4,7)\}$

(2) $\{(4,7),(2,1),(-3,6),(3,4)\}$

(3) $\{(-1,6),(1,3),(2,5),(1,7)\}$

(4) $\{(-1,2),(0,5),(5,0),(2,-1)\}$

_____

Jun '09, #19: Which statement is true about the relation shown on the graph below?

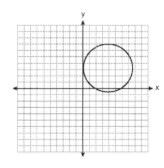

(1) It is a function because there exists one x-coordinate for each y-coordinate.
(2) It is a function because there exists one y-coordinate for each x coordinate.
(3) It is not a function because there are multiple y-values for a given x-value.
(4) It is not a function because there are multiple x-values for a given y-value.

_____

Jan '09, #30: Which graph represents a function?

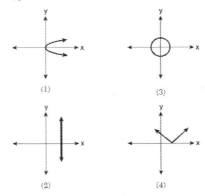

Sample #30: Which graph represents a function?

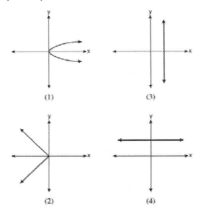

Jun '10, #13: Which graph represents a function?

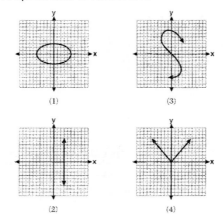

Scientific Notation

Scientific notation is _____

_____

The number has two parts:

First a number between _____

Then the number _____ raised to an _____ .

The power tells us how many places to move the decimal point if we wish to write the

number in _____ .

First change the calculator from normal mode to scientific.

Press [MODE] and move the highlighting from Normal to Sci.

Although the calculator can work with scientific notation in normal mode, in scientific mode every answer will be automatically expressed in scientific notation.

Complete the table on the next page. No calculations should be necessary. With the calculator in scientific mode,

1. Input the number.

2. Press [ENTER], and the calculator should convert the number to scientific

   notation. Write the number in scientific mode in the box below its standard

   notation.

Note that the calculator uses the notation 1.34E4 to write 1.34×10^4. You should write

your answers with _____, not with an E!!

Fill in the table below with the equivalent number in scientific notation.

All measurements are in miles. **If a box is "X-ed", leave the box below it blank.**

Planet	Distance from Sun		Distance from Earth		Mean
	Maximum	Minimum	Maximum	Minimum	Radius
Mercury	43400000	28600000	138000000	48000000	1516
Venus	67700000	66800000	162000000	24000000	3760
Earth	94500000	91400000	XXXXXXX	XXXXXXX	3959
Mars	154900000	128400000	249000000	34000000	2106
Jupiter	507400000	460100000	602000000	366000000	43441
Saturn	941100000	840400000	1031000000	743000000	36184
Uranus	1866400000	1703400000	1962000000	1604000000	15759
Neptune	2824500000	2761600000	2913000000	2676000000	15301
Sun	XXXXXXX	XXXXXXX	XXXXXXX	XXXXXXX	432500
Moon	XXXXXXX	XXXXXXX	225744	251966	1080

Operations with scientific notation:

When entering a number in scientific notation, it is best to enter it with the "E".

For example, to enter 4.382×10^5 in the TI-73,

1. Enter the 4.382.

2. Press [2ND] [∧] . Note the EE above the carat key. Only one E will appear on your screen.

3. End with the exponent on the 10.

```
4.382ᴇ5
```

When you enter numbers in this way you do not need to use parentheses to group the number.

Try this:

Find the quotient of 5.867×10^3 and -1.468×10^{-5}.

First find the quotient by entering it like this:

```
5.867*10^3/-1.46
8*10^-5
```

The result is _____ .

Now try it like this:

```
5.867ᴇ3/-1.468ᴇ-
5
```

The result is _____ .

Which is the correct answer? _____

What happened?

_____

_____

Write answers in scientific notation.

1. $1.03 \times 10^5 + 4.07 \times 10^4$

2. $6.75 \times 10^{-5} + 3.69 \times 10^{-6}$

_____

3. $4.85 \times 10^{11} + 1.98 \times 10^{10}$

4. $3.08 \times 10^{-34} + 5.97 \times 10^{-30}$

_____

5. $5.76 \times 10^{14} - 4.76 \times 10^{15}$

6. $5.82 \times 10^{-12} - 1.34 \times 10^{-13}$

_____

7. $6.05 \times 10^3 - 4.05 \times 10^3$

8. $7.15 \times 10^{-1} - 4.78 \times 10^5$

_____

9. $8.07 \times 10^{19} \bullet 1.38 \times 10^{35}$

10. $7.06 \times 10^{43} \bullet 5.99 \times 10^{-43}$

_____

11. $6.55 \times 10^6 \bullet 4.21 \times 10^7$

12. $5.07 \times 10^{-50} \bullet 2.31 \times 10^{-7}$

_____

13. $7.09 \times 10^{18} \div 4.65 \times 10^9$

14. $3.98 \times 10^{-4} \div 9.76 \times 10^8$

_____

15. $\dfrac{2.56 \times 10^{11}}{4.21 \times 10^{-7}}$

_____

16. $\dfrac{5.55 \times 10^{-16}}{4.11 \times 10^{-24}}$

_____

Regents Connection

Scientific Notation

Jun'00, #29: The distance from Earth to the imaginary planet Med is 1.7×10^7 miles. If a spaceship is capable of traveling 1420 miles per hour, how many days will it take the spaceship to reach the planet Med? Round your answer to the **nearest day**.

_____

Aug '00, #4: Expressed in decimal notation, 4.726×10^{-3} is

(1) 0.004726

(2) 0.04726

3) 472.6

4) 4,726

_____

Jan '01, #11: The distance from Earth to the Sun is approximately 93 million miles. A scientist would write that number as

(1) 9.3×10^6

(2) 9.3×10^7

3) 93×10^7

4) 93×10^{10}

_____

Aug '99, #4: Which expression is equivalent to 6.02×10^{23}?

(1) 0.602×10^{21}

(2) 60.2×10^{21}

3) 602×10^{21}

(4) 6020×10^{21}

_____

Jan '00, #18: If the number of molecules in 1 mole of a substance is 6.02×10^{23}, then the number of molecules in 100 moles is

(1) 6.02×10^{21}

(2) 6.02×10^{22}

3) 6.02×10^{24}

4) 6.02×10^{25}

_____

June '01, #8: If 0.0154 is expressed in the form 1.54×10^n, n is equal to

(1) −2

(2) 2

3) 3

4) −3

_____

<u>Jan '02, #6:</u> The approximate number of seconds in a year is $32,000,000$. When this number is written in scientific notation, the numerical value of the exponent is

(1) -7 3) 7

(2) 6   4) 8

_____

<u>June '02, #7:</u> If 3.85×10^6 is divided by 385×10^4, the result is

(1) 1   (2) 0.01   (3) 3.85×10^2 (4) 3.85×10^{10}

_____

<u>Aug '02, #10:</u> If 0.0347 is written by a scientist in the form 3.47×10^n, the value of n is

(1) -2 (2) 2   (3) 3   (4) -3

_____

<u>Jan '03, #19:</u> What is the value of $\dfrac{6.3 \times 10^8}{3 \times 10^4}$ in scientific notation?

(1) 2.1×10^{-2} (2) 2.1×10^2 (3) 2.1×10^{-4} 4) 2.1×10^4

_____

<u>June '03, #1:</u> The number 8.375×10^{-3} is equivalent to

(1) 0.0008375   2) 0.008375   (3) 0.08375 (4) 8,375

_____

<u>June '04, #29:</u> If the mass of a proton is 1.67×10^{-24} gram, what is the mass of $1,000$ protons?

(1) $1.67 \times 10^{-27} g$ (2) $1.67 \times 10^{-23} g$ (3) $1.67 \times 10^{-22} g$ (4) $1.67 \times 10^{-21} g$

_____

<u>Aug '04, #24:</u> The number 1.56×10^{-2} is equivalent to

(1) 156   (2) 0.156   (3) 0.0156   (4) 0.00156

_____

<u>June '05, #4</u>: The mass of an orchid seed is approximately 0.0000035 gram. Written in scientific notation, that mass is equivalent to 3.5×10^n. What is the value of n?

(1) -8 (2) -7 (3) -6 (4) $= 5$

<u>Aug '05, #11:</u> The expression 0.62×10^3 is equivalent to

(1) 0.062 (2) $62,000$ (3) 6.2×10^4 (4) 6.2×10^2

<u>Jan '06, #9:</u> The size of a certain type of molecule is 0.00009078 inch. If this number is expressed as 9.078×10^n, what is the value of n?

(1) -5 (2) 5 (3) -8 (4) 8

<u>June '06, #28</u>: What is the sum of 6×10^3 and 3×10^2?

(1) 6.3×10^3 (2) 9×10^5 (3) 9×10^6 (4) 18×10^5

<u>A.N.4a:</u> Express the product of each of the following in scientific notation:

a. $\left(2.0 \times 10^5\right)\left(3.0 \times 10^6\right)$

b. $\left(4.0 \times 10^7\right)\left(2.0 \times 10^{-9}\right)$

c. $\left(4.0 \times 10^{-6}\right)\left(6.0 \times 10^{-4}\right)$

<u>A.N.4b:</u> Express the quotient of each of the following in scientific notation:

a. $\dfrac{4 \times 10^5}{2 \times 10^3}$

b. $\dfrac{1.2 \times 10^8}{.2 \times 10^3}$

<u>A.N.4c:</u> If the expression $\left(6.03\times10^3\right)\left(1.35\times10^5\right)$ is evaluated, and the result is written in scientific notation, what is the value of the resultant exponent?

_____

<u>Jun '09, #27:</u> What is the product of 12 and 4.2×10^6 expressed in scientific notation?

(1) 50.4×10^6 (2) 50.4×10^7 (3) 5.04×10^6 (4) 5.04×10^7

_____

<u>Jan '09, #27:</u> What is the product of 8.4×10^8 and 4.2×10^3 written in scientific notation?

(1) 2.0×10^5 (2) 12.6×10^{11} (3) 32.28×10^{11} (4) 3.528×10^{12}

_____

<u>Sample #25:</u> What is the quotient of 8.05×10^6 and 3.5×10^2?

(1) 2.3×10^3 (2) 2.3×10^4 (3) 2.3×10^8 (4) 2.3×10^{12}

_____

Equation Solver

The TI-73 has a nifty little function called "EQUATION SOLVER".

Press and choose 6:Solver.

This can be a dangerous function or a good friend.

You should always try a problem on paper first then use SOLVER to check your answer.

Let's try it with a simple equation. Solve $5x - 2 = 13$ in the space below:

$x =$ _____

Now follow the steps below:

1. Press

2. Choose 6: Solver

3. Enter $5x - 2 = 13$. (The equal sign can be found by pressing

   then use the arrow keys to move the rectangle to the equal sign, press

    then move the rectangle to Done and press ENTER

   again.) Your screen should look like the one below.

4. Press ENTER

5. THIS IS NOT THE ANSWER!!!!! The calculator has a preset value for x at any time. The factory sets it at $x = 0$ but if you (or someone else) has used the calculator and involved x in any way it might be changed. We will call this value (whatever it is) the initial value for x.

    Use the down arrow or ENTER to move down to Solve: X.

6. Press ENTER

7. The cursor should jump back to the X= line.

8. This is the answer.

9. Did it match the answer you found on paper?

10. If yes, congratulations! You did it right!

11. If no, check both your work and what you entered in the calculator to f nd where the mistake is. Remember – the mistake isn't always what you did on paper – you must enter everything correctly on the calculator also!

Practice:
Find each solution first on paper (show your work!!) then check your answer using SOLVER.

1. $3x - 7 = 14$

2. $5x + 8 = 28$

_____

3. $8 - 4x = 28$

_____

4. $8 + 7x = 36$

_____

5. $8x - 3 = 37$

_____

6. $4 - 5x = 14$

_____

Missing Data?

Often the mean of a set of data is given and all but one of the data points. We can use SOLVER to find the missing data.

First we need to recall the basic formula.

Average = _____ = _____

Let x = the missing data and set the sum divided by the amount of data equal to the mean.

Example 1:

Meagan scored 87, 85, and 92 on the first 3 of 4 tests in the quarter. If she wants her test average to be at least 90, what must she score on the 4th test?

Then $\dfrac{87+85+92+x}{4} = 90$ or

$(87+85+92+x)/4 = 90$.

Enter this in SOLVER.

What must Meagan get on her last test?

_____

Example 2:

Andy wants to know if he can get at least an 80 in his algebra class. He knows his 4 quarterly grades: 68, 75, 70, 78. These grades and his final exam each count as $\dfrac{1}{5}$ of his final grade. Can he get an 80?

_____

What are the maximum and minimum grades Andy could have for this course?

Maximum: _____   Minimum: _____

Example 3:

Christina's current quiz average is 82 for the first 4 quizzes in the quarter. If she wants an average of 85, what must she get on the 5th and final quiz of the quarter?

_____

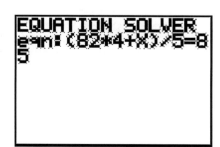

Practice:

1. In the first week of January 2007 it was unusually warm in Croghan, NY. The temperatures (in degrees Fahrenheit) for the first 6 days were:
   46°, 39°, 44°, 55°, 53°, and 55°.

   If the mean temperature for January 1 – January 7 was 47°, what was, to the nearest degree, the high temperature on January 7th?

   _____

2. Elaine knows that her first 3 test grades were 77, 85, and 82, and that her test average was 84. If there were 4 tests included in her average, what was the 4th test grade?

   _____

3. The average of 8 numbers is 124. When one more number is added the average is 121. What must this number be?

   _____

4. Twenty-two students took an earth science test with an average of 82. Two students who were absent took the test the next day. They both received the same grade and the class average changed to 83 with their grades included. What grade did they earn on the test?

   _____

5. In the first quarter Jason earned a 91 in English, 88 in Earth Science, 94 in French, and 86 in Algebra. The only other class Jason received a grade in was Social Studies. If his 1st quarter average was exactly 90, what was his Social Studies grade?

   _____

6. Work with two other students to solve the following problem:

   Cameron received a set of four grades. If the average of the first two grades is 50, the average of the second and third grades is 75, and the average of the third and fourth grades is 70, then what is the average of the first and fourth grades?

   _____

   Be prepared to present your solution to the class. The other groups in the class will also present their solutions. You will evaluate each other's solutions according to the following criteria: accuracy of the solution, clarity of the explanation, efficiency of the solution method, and creativity.

Regents Connection

Finding Missing Data

Jan '02, #30: The students in Woodland High School's meteorology class measured the noon temperature every school day for a week. Their readings for the first 4 days were Monday, 56°; Tuesday, 72°; Wednesday, 67°; and Thursday, 61°. If the mean (average) temperature for the 5 days was exactly 63°, what was the temperature on Friday?

_____

June '99, #29: The mean (average) weight of three dogs is 38 pounds. One of the dogs, Sparky, weighs 46 pounds. The other two dogs, Eddie and Sandy, have the same weight. Find Eddie's weight.

_____

Jan '00, #26: Judy needs a mean (average) score of 86 on four tests to earn a midterm grade of B. If the mean of her scores for the first three tests was 83, what is the lowest score on a 100-point scale that she can receive on the fourth test to have a midterm grade of B?

_____

Aug '01, #10: The exact average of a set of six test scores is 92. Five of these scores are 90, 98, 96, 94, and 85. What is the other test score?

   (1) 92   (2) 91   (3) 89   (4) 86

_____

Aug '99, #13: If 6 and x have the same mean (average) as 2, 4, and 24, what is the value of x?

   (1) 5   (2) 10   (3) 14   (4) 36

_____

June '02, #4: During each marking period, there are five tests. If Vanita needs a 65 average to pass this marking period and her first four grades are 60, 72, 55, and 80, what is the lowest score she can earn on the last test to have a passing grade?

    (1) 58   (2) 65   (3) 80   (4) 100

_____

Aug '02, #27: Tamika could not remember her scores from five mathematics tests. She did remember that the mean (average) was exactly 80, the median was 81, and the mode was 88. If all her scores were integers with 100 the highest score possible and 0 the lowest score possible, what was the lowest score she could have received on any one test?

_____

Math A Sample #1: For what value of x will 8 and x have the same mean (average) as 27 and 5?

    (1) 1.5   (2) 8   (3) 24   (4) 40

_____

Math A Sample #26: On his first 5 biology tests, Bob received the following scores: 72, 86, 92, 63, and 77. What test score must Bob earn on his sixth test so that his average (mean score) for all six tests will be 80%?

_____

June '00, #17: For five algebra examinations, Maria has an average of 88. What must she score on the sixth test to bring her average up to exactly 90?

    (1) 92   (2) 94   (3) 98   (4) 100

_____

Jan '04, #32: TOP Electronics is a small business with five employees. The mean (average) weekly salary for the five employees is $360. If the weekly salaries of four of the employees are $340, $340, $345, and $425, what is the salary of the fifth employee?

_____

June '04, #38: On the first six tests in her social studies course, Jerelyn's scores were 92, 78, 86, 92, 95, and 91. Determine the median and the mode of her scores. If Jerelyn took a seventh test and raised the mean of her scores exactly 1 point, what was her score on the seventh test?

_____

Regents Connection

Solving Equations

Jan '10, #9: Debbie solved the linear equation $3(x+4)-2=16$ as follows:

[Line 1]	$3(x+4)-2=16$
[Line 2]	$3(x+4)=18$
[Line 3]	$3x+4=18$
[Line 4]	$3x=14$
[Line 5]	$x=4\frac{2}{3}$

She made an error between lines

(1) 1 and 2   (2) 2 and 3   (3) 3 and 4   (4) 4 and 5

_____

Jun '09, #7: Which value of x is the solution of the equation $\dfrac{2x}{3}+\dfrac{x}{6}=5$?

(1) 6   (2) 10   (3) 15   (4) 30

_____

Jan '09, #18: What is the value of x in the equation $\dfrac{2}{x}-3=\dfrac{26}{x}$?

(1) -8 (2) $-\dfrac{1}{8}$ (3) $\dfrac{1}{8}$ (4) 8

_____

Aug '08, #1: Which value of p is the solution of $5p-1=2p+20$?

(1) $\dfrac{19}{7}$ (2) $\dfrac{19}{3}$ (3) 3   (4) 7

_____

Absolute Value

The absolute value of a number is defined as _____

_____

_____

$$-n \qquad\qquad 0 \qquad\qquad n$$

Because it is a _____ , it is **always** _____ .

(The distance from _____ to 0 is the same as the distance from _____ to 0 .)

The standard notation for the absolute value of a number " n " is _____ .

On the TI-73 we do not have this notation available. Instead we will use _____ .

Example:

Find $\left|3x-2\right|$ for $x=-5$.

1. As we did for evaluating expressions, **first store –5 to** x .

2. Now press **MATH** .

3. Arrow over to NUM.

4. Choose 1:abs.

5. Enter your expression.

6. Close the parentheses and press **ENTER** .

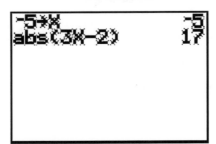

So, the absolute value of $3x-2$ when $x=-5$ is _____ .

Practice:

Evaluate each of the given absolute value expressions for the specified value of x.

1. $\left|1-4x\right|$ for $x=6$ _____

2. $\left|3x+5\right|$ for $x=-3$ _____

3. $\left|-2x+10\right|$ for $x=-12$ _____

4. $\left|\dfrac{2}{5}x-11\right|$ for $x=-10$ _____

5. $9-\left|\dfrac{1}{2}-\dfrac{3}{4}x\right|$ for $x=8$ _____

6. $\left|-9x+3\right|-\left|2x+4\right|$ for $x=-3$ _____

7. $\left|3x-7\right|-15$ for $x=-1$ _____

8. $3x-\left|7-x\right|$ for $x=5$ _____

9. $\left|3x^2-5x+2\right|$ for $x=-2$ _____

10. $\left|-x^2+3x-7\right|$ for $x=10$ _____

11. $\left|-2x^2+3x-12\right|$ for $x=6$ _____

12. $\left|\dfrac{2-x}{-3}\right|$ for $x=5$ _____

13. $\dfrac{\left|2-x\right|}{-3}$ for $x=5$ _____

14. Your answers for #12 and #13 should be different. The expressions appear almost identical. Explain why the answers are different.

_____

_____

_____

Graphing Absolute Value

In this lesson we will practice graphing absolute value functions and try to determine how the parts of the equation affect the finished product.

To graph absolute value functions we will need to remember how to find absolute value on the calculator. We can find it by pressing _____, moving over to _____ , and choosing _____ .

Or, if we really can't remember how to get there, we can resort to finding it in the _____ . (_____)

Let's set up a general equation so that we can refer to the parts of the equation more easily:

$$y = |ax + b| + c$$

To see what the most basic absolute value equation looks like, graph $y = |x|$ on the graphing calculator and sketch the screen in the box below.

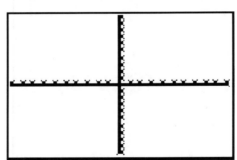

What do you notice about the values of y? _____

What makes this equation different than others you have graphed?

_____

_____

In this lesson you may make "quick" sketches, but be sure the turning point of the equation is accurately placed!

Graph and sketch the following equations.

1. $y = |2x|$

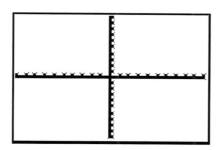

2. $y = |5x|$

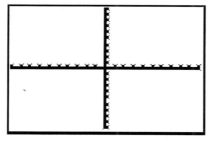

3. $y = |10x|$

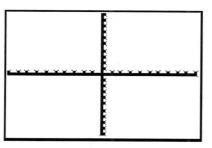

4. $y = \left|\dfrac{1}{2}x\right|$

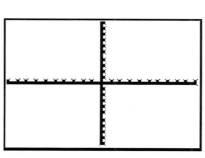

What conclusion can you make about the effect that "a" has on the appearance of the graph of the absolute value equation?

_____

_____

_____

_____

5. $y = |.1x|$

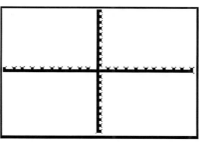

6. $y = |x - 1|$

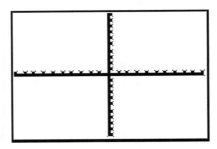

7. $y = |x + 1|$

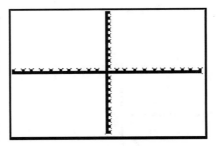

8. $y = |x - 3|$

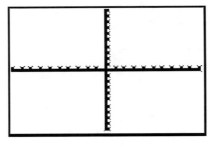

9. $y = |x + 3|$

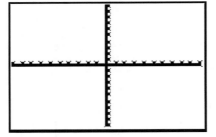

What conclusion can you make about the effect that "b" has on the appearance of the graph of the absolute value equation?

_____

_____

_____

10. $y = |x - 5|$

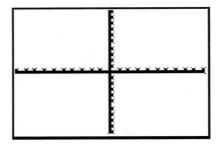

11. $y = |x + 5|$

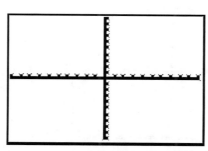

12. $y = |x| - 1$

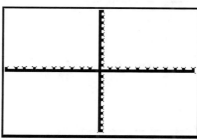

13. $y = |x| + 4$

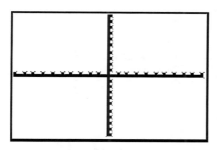

What conclusion can you make about the effect that "c" has on the appearance of the graph of the absolute value equation?

_____

_____

_____

_____

14. $y = |x| - 5$

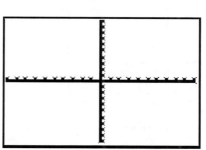

15. $y = |x| + 8$

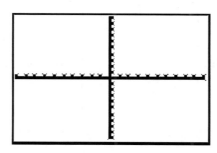

Try these:

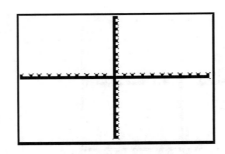

16. $y = 3|x|$

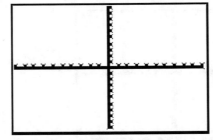

17. $y = -|x|$

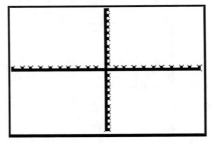

18. $y = -3|x + 1|$

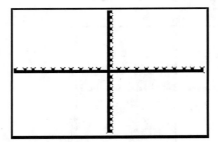

19. $y = -|2x + 5| + 3$

Can you find the equation that matches these graphs?

20.

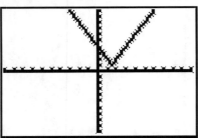

21.

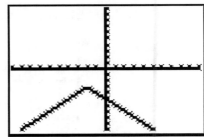

_____   _____

Regents Connection

Absolute Value

A.CM.3c

If $a \lozenge b = |a - b|$, then what is the value of $2 \lozenge 3$?

_____

A.N.6a

Evaluate the following expressions

$$\left|-153\right|$$

_____

$$\left|23\right| + \left|-9\right|$$

_____

A.G.4a

Identify what type of function the equation represents. Draw the graph of the equation.

$$y = \left| x + 4 \right|$$

_____

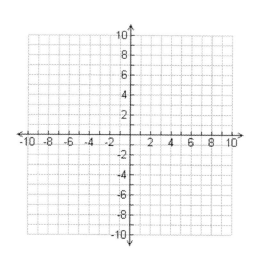

<u>Jan '10, #17</u>: The graph of the equation $y = |x|$ is shown in the diagram below.

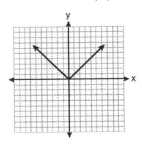

Which diagram could represent a graph of the equation $y = a|x|$ when $-1 < a < 0$?

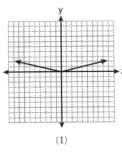

(1)

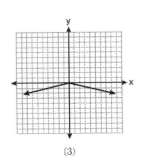

(3)

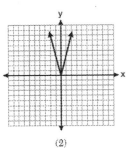

(2)

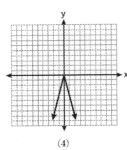

(4)

<u>Aug '09, #25</u>: Which equation is represented by the graph below?

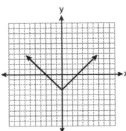

(1) $y = x^2 - 3$

(3) $y = |x| - 3$

(2) $y = (x-3)^2$

(4) $y = |x-3|$

<u>Sample #22</u>: The diagram below shows the graph of $y = |x - 3|$.

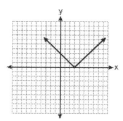

Which diagram shows the graph of $y = -|x - 3|$?

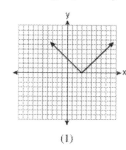

(1)

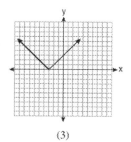

(3)

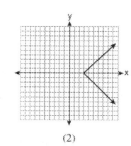

(2)

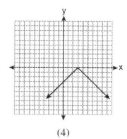

(4)

Jun '10, #35: Graph and label the following equations on the set of axes below.

$$y = |x|$$

$$y = \left| \frac{1}{2}x \right|$$

Explain how decreasing the coefficient affects the graph of the equation $y = |x|$.

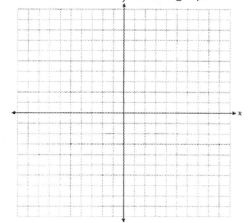

Using the Graphing Calculator to:

Construct Good Responses to Quadratic Questions

First:

A quadratic equation is:

_____

_____

The graph of a quadratic equation is called a _____ .

Did you know:

1. Given a quadratic equation, we can find the roots using equation solver?

2. Given the roots of an equation, we can find an equation that fits these roots?

3. If we can find the roots, we can construct an algebraic response?

4. Given three points, we can find the quadratic equation that fits these points?

5. We can find the roots of an equation graphically?

6. We can change the window to fit the dimensions of a pre-labeled grid?

1. Finding the roots in equation solver.

   The only problem with using SOLVER to find roots (solutions) for a quadratic equation is that SOLVER will give us only one answer. Most quadratics have

   _____ .

   Integrated Algebra (Algebra 1) questions will normally have "small' roots. After you have found the first solution, change "x=" to 10 or -10 to find the second root.

   Let's try a couple:
   Find the solution(s):

   a. $0 = x^2 - 2x - 3$ _____

   b. $0 = x^2 - 6x - 16$ _____

Before moving on to the rest of the list we will take a detour into how to graph quadratic equations.

Graphing Quadratic Equations

Picture the path a lobbed baseball takes, or the shape of the St. Louis Arch. These are

_____ .

These would be called _____ parabolas.

Now picture the curve of a hammock, or a bowl or cup that that has been cut in half from the top, or even a smile. These are also _____ .

These would be called _____ parabolas.

Some people like to use rhyming words to help remember these terms:

_____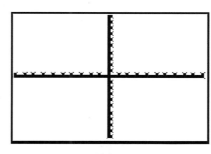

or

_____

Let's do a little exploration to determine what makes a parabola concave up or concave down.

In a standard window graph the following equations by entering them in Y_1, one at a time, and sketching your screen in the space provided.

a. $y = x^2 - 3x + 2$

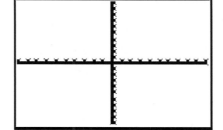

b. $y = -x^2 - 3x + 2$

c. $y = -2x^2 - 3x + 1$

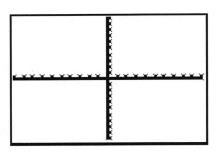

d. $2x^2 - 3x + 1$

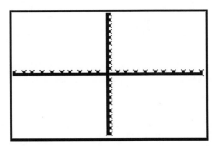

e. $y = 3x^2 + x - 2$

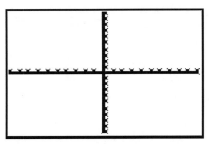

f. $y = -3x^2 + x - 2$

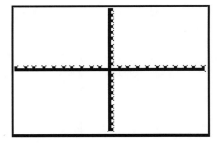

What conclusion can you make about the part of the quadratic equation that determines whether the parabola is concave up or concave down?

_____

_____

_____

Now we have to get a little picky. It's time to transfer our graph to a grid.

For every graph that is not a straight line you must plot _____ !

For parabolas, these will be particular points and will usually require a 4th point to be plotted to get all these important ones in.

You must plot:

1. Where the parabola meets the y-axis. This is called the

    _____ and is easy to find. On the y-axis x is equal to

    _____ . If you substitute zero for x in the equation $y = ax^2 + bx + c$,

    what is left? _____ This is true no matter what

    a and b are! So plot the point _____ .

2. Where the parabola meets the x-axis. These are called the _____ .
    On the x-axis y is equal to _____ , so these are also the solution(s) to

    the equation _____ . You could use solver, but for this

    course it is probably much quicker to use the _____ .

    Go to the TABLE (press [2ND] [GRAPH]). Find the x-value(s) that

    correspond to zeroes in the Y column. There will usually be two, but sometimes only

    one. Plot the points _____ .

3. Where the parabola _____ . This is called the

    _____ . This will always be exactly

    _____ . (Or on the root

    itself if there is only one.) If you found two values of x that corresponded to zeroes

    in the Y column, find the x-value exactly half-way between the two, in other words,

    _____ . If this number is an integer

    you can look up the corresponding y-value in the table. Otherwise, the quickest

    way to find it is to press [TRACE] and enter the x-value. Plot this point on

    your grid.

4. If the parabola only had one root, choose one more x-value and its

    corresponding y to plot. This x should lie on the opposite side of the turning point

    from the y-axis.

With your 3 or 4 points plotted join them with a smooth curve. Parabolas are not

_____ or _____ on the top! They should look

_____ !

Practice: Graph each of the quadratic equations by graphing the equation on your TI-73, sketching your screen, then transferring the graph to the grid provided. Be sure to label points and axes!

a. $y = x^2 + 2x - 3$

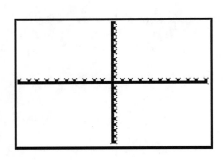

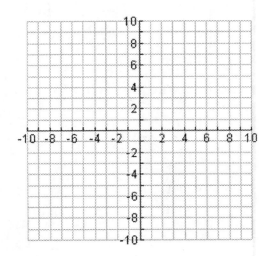

y-intercept: _____

root(s): _____

turning point: _____

b. $y = -x^2 - 2x + 8$

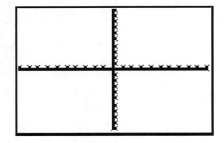

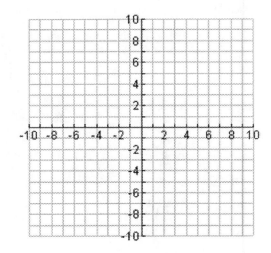

y-intercept: _____

root(s): _____

turning point: _____

c. $y = x^2 + 3x - 4$

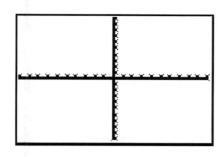

y-intercept: _____

root(s): _____

turning point: _____

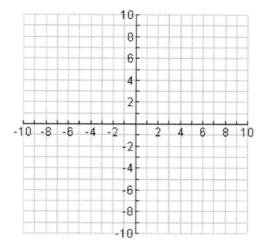

d. $y = -x^2 + 6x - 9$

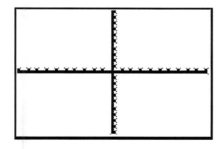

y-intercept: _____

root(s): _____

turning point: _____

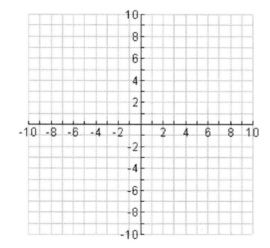

Back to our list of "Can Do's":

2. Once you've found the roots, you can work backward to find the factors. Every quadratic equation should have _____ . Factors are

_____

_____

    a. Find the factors of the $x^2 + 2x - 3$ by using the roots. (Remember, you had to find the roots of the equation $y = x^2 + 2x - 3$ to graph this equation!)

                                                               _____

    b. Find the factors of $-x^2 - 2x + 8$ by using the roots.

                                                               _____

    c. Find the factors of $x^2 + 3x - 4$ using the roots.

                                                               _____

    d. Find the factors of $-x^2 + 6x - 9$ using the roots.

                                                               _____

3. Often a long answer question will require you to write out an algebraic response to a quadratic solution. It's good to be able to do this without the calculator, but if you really draw a blank we can use what we learned in 1 and 2 and with a little more filling in, we will have our algebraic answer.

    a. Write an algebraic solution to the following equation:

$$0 = x^2 + 4x - 12$$

b. Write an algebraic solution to the following equation:

$$0 = x^2 + x - 2$$

4. If you are given the graph of a quadratic equation and can identify at least 3 points, you can use a method very similar to the linear regressions we used to find the equation of a line.

The points $(-2,0),(0,-6),$ and $(3,0)$ are points on the parabola shown in the graph below.

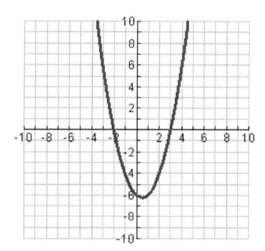

a. Press [LIST]

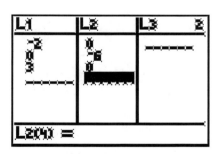

b. Enter the points in L1 and L2 by placing all the x's in L1 and all the y's in L2. Be sure that the ordered pairs are lined up together.

c. Press [2ND] [LIST] .

d. Go over to CALC.

e. Choose 6:QuadReg. If your data is in L1 and L2 and in the correct order, press [ENTER] .

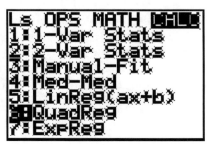

If the data is located somewhere else you will need to tack on the list names after the QuadReg.

f. The screen below should appear.

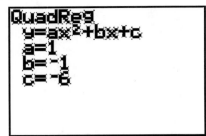

g. Replace the corresponding values in the general form of the quadratic equation to find that the graph is of the equation:

$$y = x^2 - x - 6$$

**Notice how the ones do not appear and the negatives become subtraction!!

Practice: Use a quadratic regression to find the quadratic equations whose graphs pass through the given points.

i. $(-1,12)$, $(0,6)$, $(1,2)$ _____

ii. $(-2,-7)$, $(-1,-7)$, $(2,17)$ _____

iii. $(-1,1)$, $(0,5)$, $(3,-19)$ _____

iv. $(-2,-3)$, $(1,12)$, $(3,32)$ _____

v. $(-1,-7)$, $(0,3)$, $(2,-25)$ _____

5. If you are given a grid to graph your parabola, ALWAYS!!! check to see if it pre-labeled. If it is, press WINDOW and change the dimensions and scale to match the labeling on the grid.
    a. Try the regents question below:

Greg is in a car at the top of a roller-coaster ride. The distance, d, of the car from the ground as the car descends is determined by the equation $d = 144 - 16t^2$, where t is the number of seconds it takes the car to travel down to each point on the ride. How many seconds will it take Greg to reach the ground?

For an algebraic solution show your work here.

For a graphic solution show your work here.

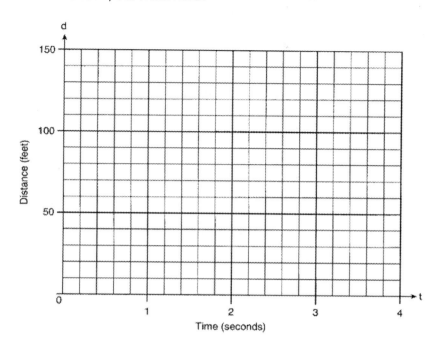

b. Now try this one:

An architect is designing a museum entranceway in the shape of a parabolic arch represented by the equation $y = -x^2 + 20x$, where $0 \leq x \leq 20$ and all dimensions are expressed in feet. On the accompanying set of axes, sketch a graph of the arch and determine its maximum height, in feet.

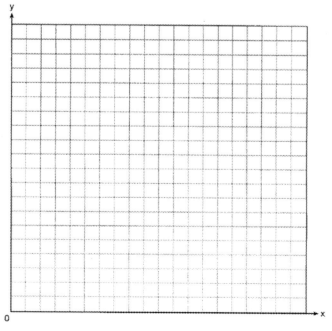

Regents Connection

Factoring and Solving Quadratic Equations

<u>Aug '01, #18:</u> What is the solution set of $m^2 - 3m - 10 = 0$?

    (1) $\{5, -2\}$ (3) $\{3, -10\}$

    (2) $\{2, -5\}$ (4) $\{3, 10\}$

<u>Jan '02, #15:</u> What is the solution set of the equation $3x^2 = 48$?

    (1) $\{-2, -8\}$ (3) $\{4, -4\}$

    (2) $\{2, 8\}$ (4) $\{4, 4\}$

<u>Jan '01, #5:</u> One of the factors of $4x^2 - 9$ is

    (1) $(x + 3)$ (3) $(4x - 3)$

    (2) $(2x + 3)$ (4) $(x - 3)$

<u>Aug '00, #12:</u> The solution set for the equation $x^2 - 2x - 15 = 0$ is

    (1) $\{5, 3\}$ (3) $\{-5, 3\}$

    (2) $\{5, -3\}$ (4) $\{-5, -3\}$

<u>Aug '99, #26:</u> Solve for x: $x^2 + 3x - 40 = 0$

<u>Jan '00, #4:</u> Which expression is a factor of $x^2 + 2x - 15$?

    (1) $(x - 3)$ (3) $(x + 15)$

    (2) $(x + 3)$ (4) $(x - 5)$

<u>June '01, #9</u>: Factor completely: $3x^2 - 27$

(1) $3(x-3)^2$ (3) $3(x+3)(x-3)$

(2) $3(x^2 - 27)$ (4) $(3x+3)(x-9)$

_____

<u>June '01, #31</u>: Find three consecutive odd integers such that the product of the first and the second exceeds the third by 8.

_____

<u>Jan '01, #31</u>: Solve algebraically for x: $\dfrac{1}{x} = \dfrac{x+1}{6}$

_____

<u>Aug '01, #3</u>: Written in simplest factored form, the binomial $2x^2 - 50$ can be expressed as

(1) $2(x-5)(x-5)$ (3) $(x-5)(x+5)$

(2) $2(x-5)(x+5)$ (4) $2x(x-50)$

_____

<u>June '02, #6</u>: Which expression is a factor of $n^2 + 3n - 54$?

(1) $n+6$ (3) $n-9$

(2) $n^2 + 9$ (4) $n+9$

_____

<u>June '02, #29</u>: Solve for x: $x^2 + 3x - 28 = 0$

_____

<u>Jan '02, #1</u>: Expressed in factored form, the binominal $4a^2 - 9b^2$ is equivalent to

(1) $(2a-3b)(2a-3b)$ (3) $(4a-3b)(a+3b)$

(2) $(2a+3b)(2a-3b)$ (4) $(2a-9b)(2a+b)$

_____

<u>Jan '03, #18:</u> What are the factors of $x^2 - 10x - 24$?

(1) $(x-4)(x+6)$ (2) $(x-4)(x-6)$ (3) $(x-12)(x+2)$ (4) $(x+12)(x-2)$

_____

<u>Jan '03, #26:</u> Three brothers have ages that are consecutive even integers. The product of the first and third boys' ages is 20 more than twice the second boy's age. Find the age of each of the three boys.

_____

<u>June '03, #13:</u> What is the solution set of the equation $x^2 - 5x - 24 = 0$?

(1) $\{-3,8\}$ (2) $\{-3,-8\}$ (3) $\{3,8\}$ (4) $\{3,-8\}$

_____

<u>Jan '04, #14:</u> What is a common factor of $x^2 - 9$ and $x^2 - 5x + 6$?

(1) $x+3$ (2) $x-3$ (3) $x-2$ (4) x^2

_____

<u>June '04, #21:</u> If $3x$ is one factor of $3x^2 - 9x$, what is the other factor?

(1) $3x$ (2) $x^2 - 6x$ (3) $x-3$ (4) $x+3$

_____

<u>June '04, #30:</u> If $(x-4)$ is a factor of $x^2 - x - w = 0$, then the value of w is

(1) 12   (2) −12   (3) 3   (4) −3

_____

Sample #26: The length of a rectangular window is 5 feet more than its width, w. The area of the window is 36 feet. Which equation could be used to find the dimensions of the window?

$$(1) \quad w^2 + 5w + 36 = 0 \qquad\qquad (3) \quad w^2 - 5w + 36 = 0$$

$$(2) \quad w^2 - 5w - 36 = 0 \qquad\qquad (4) \quad w^2 + 5w - 36 = 0$$

_____

Sample #39: Solve for x: $\dfrac{x+1}{x} = \dfrac{-7}{x-12}$

_____

June '08, #4:
Factored, the expression $16x^2 - 25y^2$ is equivalent to

$$(1) \quad (4x - 5y)(4x + 5y) \qquad\qquad (3) \quad (8x - 5y)(8x + 5y)$$

$$(2) \quad (4x - 5y)(4x - 5y) \qquad\qquad (4) \quad (8x - 5y)(8x - 5y)$$

_____

Aug '08, #6: Factored completely, the expression $2x^2 + 10x - 12$ is equivalent to

$$(1) \quad 2(x - 6)(x + 1) \qquad\qquad (3) \quad 2(x + 2)(x + 3)$$

$$(2) \quad 2(x + 6)(x - 1) \qquad\qquad (4) \quad 2(x - 2)(x - 3)$$

_____

Jan '10, #22: If Ann correctly factors an expression that is the difference of two perfect squares, her factors could be

$$(1) \quad (2x + y)(x - 2y) \qquad\qquad (3) \quad (x - 4)(x - 4)$$
$$(2) \quad (2x + 3y)(2x - 3y) \qquad\qquad (4) \quad (2y - 5)(y - 5)$$

_____

<u>Jan '10, #28</u>: What is the solution set of $\dfrac{x+2}{x-2} = \dfrac{-3}{x}$?

(1) $\{-2,3\}$ (2) $\{-3,-2\}$ (3) $\{-1,6\}$ (4) $\{-6,1\}$

_____

<u>Jan '10, #34</u>: Find the roots of the equation $x^2 - x = 6$ algebraically.

_____

<u>Jan '10, #39</u>: find three consecutive positive even integers such that the product of the second and third integers is twenty more than ten times the first integer. [Only an algebraic solution can receive full credit.]

_____

<u>Aug '09, #2</u>: Which expression is equivalent to $9x^2 - 16$?

(1) $(3x+4)(3x-4)$ (3) $(3x+8)(3x-8)$

(2) $(3x-4)(3x-4)$ (4) $(3x-8)(3x-8)$

_____

<u>Aug '09, #18</u>: Which value of x makes the expression $\dfrac{x^2-9}{x^2+7x+10}$ undefined?

(1) -5 (2) 2   (3) 3   (4) -3

_____

<u>Aug '09, #21</u>: The solution to the equation $x^2 - 6x = 0$ is

(1) 0, only   (2) 6, only   (3) 0 and 6 (4) $\pm\sqrt{6}$

_____

<u>Aug '09, #34</u>: Find algebraically the equation of the axis of symmetry and the coordinates of the vertex of the parabola whose equation is $y = -2x^2 - 8x + 3$.

_____

_____

<u>Jun '09, #2</u>: What are the roots of the equation $x^2 - 7x + 6 = 0$?

(1) 1 and 7   (3) −1 and −6
(2) −1 and 7   (4) 1 and 6

_____

<u>Jun '09, #21</u>: Which expression represents $\dfrac{x^2 - 2x - 15}{x^2 + 3x}$ in simplest form?

(1) −5   (2) $\dfrac{x-5}{x}$ (3) $\dfrac{-2x-5}{x}$ (4) $\dfrac{-2x-15}{3x}$

_____

<u>Jun '09, #32</u>: Factor completely: $4x^2 - 36x$

_____

<u>Jan '09, #9</u>: The expression $9x^2 - 100$ is equivalent to

(1) $(9x - 10)(x + 10)$ (3) $(3x - 100)(3x - 1)$
(2) $(3x - 10)(3x + 10)$ (4) $(9x - 100)(x + 1)$

_____

<u>Jan '09, #14</u>: What are the roots of the equation $x^2 - 10x + 21 = 0$?

(1) 1 and 21   (3) 3 and 7
(2) −5 and −5   (4) −3 and −7

_____

<u>Jan '09, #25</u>: The function $y = \dfrac{x}{x^2 - 9}$ is undefined when the value of x is

(1) 0 or 3   (2) 3 or −3   (3) 3, only   (4) −3, only

_____

<u>Jan '09, #35</u>: Perform the indicated operation and simplify: $\dfrac{3x+6}{4x+12} \div \dfrac{x^2-4}{x+3}$

<u>Aug '08, #21</u>: Which expression represents $\dfrac{25x-125}{x^2-25}$ in simplest form?

(1) $\dfrac{5}{x}$ (2) $\dfrac{-5}{x}$ (3) $\dfrac{25}{x-5}$ (4) $\dfrac{25}{x+5}$

<u>Aug '08, #26</u>: What is the product of $\dfrac{4x}{x-1}$ and $\dfrac{x^2-1}{3x+3}$ in simplest form?

(1) $\dfrac{4x}{3}$ (2) $\dfrac{4x^2}{3}$ (3) $\dfrac{4x^2}{3(x+1)}$ (4) $\dfrac{4(x+1)}{3}$

<u>Jun '08, #15</u>: What is the product of $\dfrac{x^2-1}{x+1}$ and $\dfrac{x+3}{3x-3}$ expressed in simplest form?

(1) x (2) $\dfrac{x}{3}$ (3) $x+3$ (4) $\dfrac{x+3}{3}$

<u>Jun '08, #26</u>: Which value of x is a solution of $\dfrac{5}{x} = \dfrac{x+13}{6}$?

(1) -2 (2) -3 (3) -10 (4) -15

<u>Sample #6</u>: The expression x^2-16 is equivalent to

(1) $(x+2)(x-8)$ (3) $(x+4)(x-4)$

(2) $(x-2)(x+8)$ (4) $(x+8)(x-8)$

<u>Sample #28</u>: for which value of x is $\dfrac{x-3}{x^2-4}$ undefined?

    (1) -2 (2) 0 (3) 3 (4) 4

<u>Jun '10, #14</u>: The algebraic expression $\dfrac{x-2}{x^2-9}$ is undefined when x is

    (1) 0 (2) 2 (3) 3 (4) 9

<u>Jun '10, #20</u>: When 36 is subtracted from the square of a number, the result is five times the number. What is the positive solution?

    (1) 9 (2) 6 (3) 3 (4) 4

<u>Jun '10, #27</u>: Factored completely, the expression $3x^2-3x-18$ is equivalent to

    (1) $3\left(x^2-x-6\right)$ (3) $(3x-9)(x+2)$

    (2) $3(x-3)(x+2)$ (4) $(3x+6)(x-3)$

<u>Jun '10, #37</u>: Express in simplest form: $\dfrac{x^2+9x+14}{x^2-49} \div \dfrac{3x+6}{x^2+x-56}$

Regents Connection

Graphing Quadratic Equations

Sample #17: Which type of graph is shown in the diagram below?

(1) absolute value   (3) linear

(2) exponential   (4) quadratic

_____

Jan '10, #15: What is the equation of the axis of symmetry of the parabola shown in the diagram below?

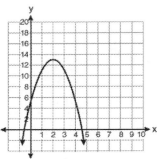

(1) $x = -0.5$ (2) $x = 2$ (3) $x = 4.5$ (4) $x = 13$

_____

Jun '09, #18: What are the vertex and axis of symmetry of the parabola $y = x^2 - 16x + 63$?

(1) vertex: $(8, -1)$; axis of symmetry: $x = 8$

(2) vertex: $(8, 1)$; axis of symmetry: $x = 8$

(3) vertex: $(-8, -1)$; axis of symmetry: $x = -8$

(4) vertex: $(-8, 1)$; axis of symmetry: $x = -8$

_____

<u>Aug '99, #33:</u> An arch is built so that it is 6 feet wide at the base. Its shape can be represented by a parabola with the equation $y = -2x^2 + 12x$, where y is the height of the arch.

a Graph the parabola from $x = 0$ to $x = 6$ on the grid below.

b Determine the maximum height, y, of the arch. _____

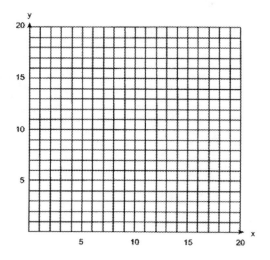

<u>June '02, #35:</u> A rocket is launched from the ground and follows a parabolic path represented by the equation $y = -x^2 + 10x$. At the same time, a flare is launched from a height of 10 feet and follows a straight path represented by the equation $y = -x + 10$.

Using the accompanying set of axes, graph the equations that represent the paths of the rocket and the flare, and find the coordinates of the point or points where the paths intersect.

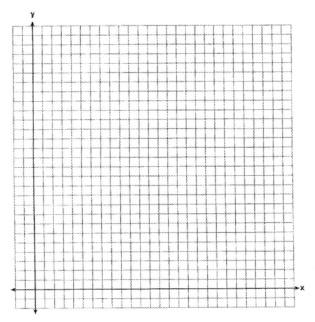

<u>June '03, #33:</u> An architect is designing a museum entranceway in the shape of a parabolic arch represented by the equation $y = -x^2 + 20x$, where $0 \le x \le 20$ and all dimensions are expressed in feet. On the accompanying set of axes, sketch a graph of the arch and determine its maximum height, in feet.

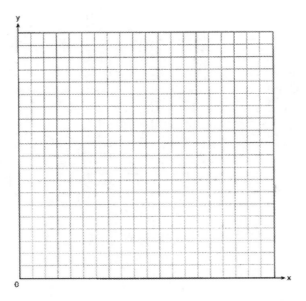

<u>June '08, #11:</u> What are the vertex and the axis of symmetry of the parabola shown in the diagram below?

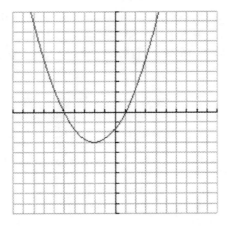

(1) The vertex is $(-2, -3)$, and the axis of symmetry is $x = -2$.

(2) The vertex is $(-2, -3)$, and the axis of symmetry is $y = -2$.

(3) The vertex is $(-3, -2)$, and the axis of symmetry is $y = -2$.

(4) The vertex is $(-3, -2)$, and the axis of symmetry is $x = -2$.

<u>Aug '09, #16</u>: The equation $y = -x^2 - 2x + 8$ is graphed on the set of axes below.

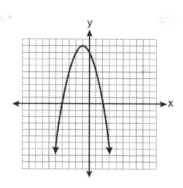

Based on the graph, what are the roots of the equation $-x^2 - 2x + 8 = 0$?

(1) 8 and 0   (3) 9 and −1
(2) 2 and −4   (4) 4 and −2

<u>Jun '09, #24</u>: The equation $y = x^2 + 3x - 18$ is graphed on the set of axes below.

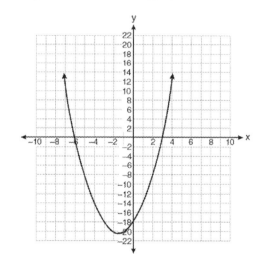

Based on this graph, what are the roots of the equation $x^2 + 3x - 18 = 0$?

(1) −3 and 6   (3) 3 and −6
(2) 0 and −18   (4) 3 and −18

<u>Jan '09, #16</u>: Which equation represents the axis of symmetry of the graph of the parabola below?

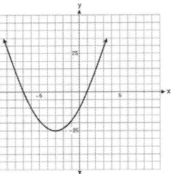

    (1) $y = -3$ (2) $x = -3$ (3) $y = -25$ (4) $x = -25$

<u>Jun '08, #29</u>: Consider the graph of the equation $y = ax^2 + bx + c$, when $a \neq 0$. If a is multiplied by 3, what is true of the graph of the resulting parabola?

    (1) The vertex is 3 units above the vertex of the original parabola.
    (2) The new parabola is 3 units to the right of the original parabola.
    (3) The new parabola is wider than the original parabola.
    (4) The new parabola is narrower than the original parabola.

<u>Aug '08, #13</u>: A swim team member performs a dive from a 14-foot-high springboard. The parabola below shows the path of her dive.

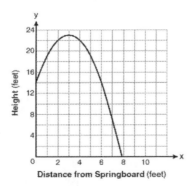

Which equation represents the axis of symmetry?

    (1) $x = 3$ (2) $y = 3$ (3) $x = 23$ (4) $y = 23$

<u>Jun '08, #36</u>: Graph the equation $y = x^2 - 2x - 3$ on the accompanying set of axes. Using the graph, determine the roots of the equation $x^2 - 2x - 3 = 0$.

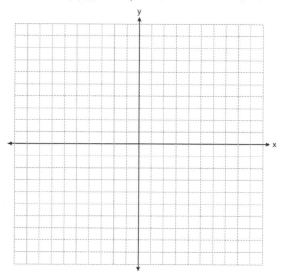

<u>Jun '10, #5</u>: What are the vertex and axis of symmetry of the parabola shown in the diagram below?

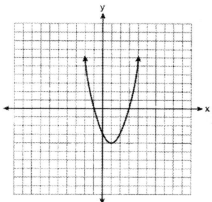

(1) vertex: $(1, -4)$; axis of symmetry: $x = 1$

(2) vertex: $(1, -4)$; axis of symmetry: $x = -4$

(3) vertex: $(-4, 1)$; axis of symmetry: $x = 1$

(4) vertex: $(-4, 1)$; axis of symmetry: $x = -4$

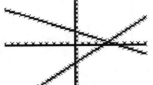

Solving Systems Of Equations

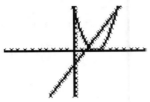

A system of equations is

_____

_____

When we graph a system of equations the solution appears as their _____ or

_____ of _____ .

With the TI-73 the best method for finding the solution(s) will be to use the _____.

While the table won't work efficiently for all systems, for Integrated Algebra we only need

to be concerned with _____ (_____) solutons so

the table will be sufficient for our needs.

There are two types of systems that we will solve:

     1. _____

     2. _____

First the Linear-Linear:

When two lines are graphed in the same plane there are two possibilities:

     1. _____

     2. _____

When there is a point of intersection, this point is the _____ to the

_____ .

In a table we will look for the x-value that has matching Y1 and Y2 values.

Consider the table below.

X	Y1	Y2
0	-8	
1	-4	
2	0	
3	4	
4	8	
5	12	
6	16	

X=0

Notice that there is exactly one x-value that has the same value for y in both the Y1 and Y2 columns. This x-value is _____ . The y-value that corresponds to this x-value is _____ . Therefore the solution to the system is _____ .

Let's try it on your TI-73.

Let $Y_1 = \dfrac{4}{3}x + \dfrac{11}{3}$ and $Y_2 = \dfrac{2}{5}x + \dfrac{23}{5}$. Find the solution to the system Y1, Y2.

1. Enter the equations in Y1 and Y2.

2. Press 2ND GRAPH .

3. Estimate the solution by graphing in a standard window and sketching your screen below. What appears to be the point of intersection?

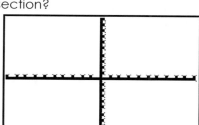

_____

4. Copy the values for Y1 and Y2 in the table below.

X	Y1	Y2
-3		
-2		
-1		
0		
1		
2		
3		

5. At what x-value do Y1 and Y2 match?

_____

6. What is this matching y-value?

_____

7. What is the solution to the system?

_____

What if the solution is a little harder to find?

Enter the following equations in Y1 and Y2: $Y_1 = \dfrac{1}{3}x - \dfrac{56}{3}$ and $Y_2 = -\dfrac{9}{8}x + \dfrac{21}{2}$

Graph the functions in a standard window. What do you notice about the graph?

_____

_____

Below is the table for this system from $x = -3$ to $x = 3$.

We could aimlessly scroll up and down the table to find the solution or we could take just a minute to be sure that we are going the right direction.

Are the Y1 and Y2 values closer together at $x = 3$ or at $x = -3$? _____

Then this is the direction we should scroll to find the solution. Find it now.

_____

Try the same method with this system:

$$y = 2x - 12$$
$$y = 2x + 25$$

What do you notice about the relationships between each pair of y-values?

_____

_____

What is causing this?

_____

_____

So we can conclude that

_____

_____

_____

Practice: Graph each pair of equations in a standard window. Sketch the screen in the space provided. Find the solution to each linear system if it exists.

**You may need to solve for y before entering the system in the TI-73.

1. $y = -2x + 10$

      $y = x + 4$

      _____

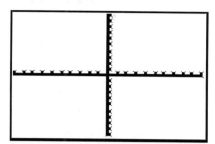

2. $y = \dfrac{13}{4}x - \dfrac{19}{2}$

      $y = -\dfrac{5}{4}x - \dfrac{1}{2}$

      _____

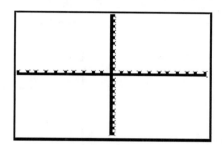

3. $y = -\dfrac{1}{9}x - \dfrac{52}{9}$

      $y = x + 2$

      _____

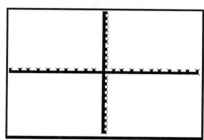

4. $y = \dfrac{5}{8}x + \dfrac{69}{8}$

      $y = \dfrac{1}{4}x + \dfrac{33}{4}$

      _____

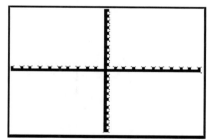

5. $y = \dfrac{4}{3}x - \dfrac{4}{3}$

      $y = -\dfrac{1}{6}x + \dfrac{55}{6}$

      _____

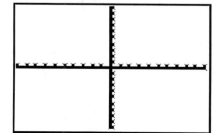

6. $y = \dfrac{3}{5}x - 7$

        $y = \dfrac{3}{5}x + 4$

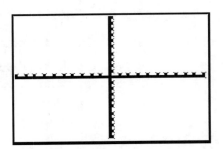

_____

7. $-3x + 8y = 6$

        $x + 4y = 18$

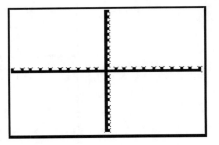

_____

8. $5x + 3y = 2$

        $-10x + y = 24$

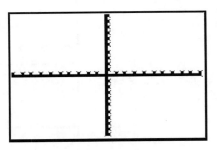

_____

9. $-7x + 5y = 20$

        $4x + 2y = 8$

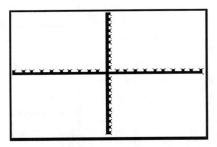

_____

10. $3x - 2y = 4$

        $6x - 4y = 10$

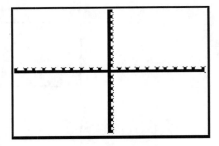

_____

Quadratic-Linear Systems:

While linear-linear systems had two possible outcomes, quadratic-linear systems have

_____ possible outcomes:

1. The outcome you will encounter most often is _____ solutions, or

   _____points of _____ .

2. It is possible to have only _____ solution. We say that the line is

   _____ to the parabola or it just

   _____ it. This will appear as _____ point

   of _____ .

3. The third possibility is that there are _____ solutions or _____ points of

   intersection.

_____ the system will be the quickest way to see which

of the cases a particular system falls into.

Case 1: Graph the following system and sketch the screen in the space provided.

$$y = -3x^2 + 8x + 2$$

$$y = 2x - 7$$

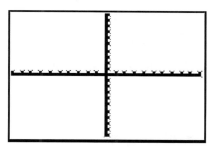

How many points of intersection are there between the line and the parabola? _____

Then there are _____ solutions to the system of equations.

Again the table will be sufficient for finding these solutions. It is important to know with

quadratic-linear systems how many solutions we are looking for so graphing first is

encouraged!

Use the table at the right to determine the solutions to

the system.

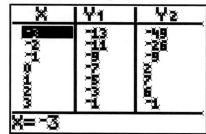

_____ and _____

Case 2: Graph the system below on your TI-73 and sketch the screen in the space provided.

$$y = x^2 + 2x - 8$$

$$y = -9$$

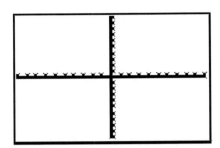

How many points of intersection do there appear to be between the parabola and the line? _____

Then there is _____ solution to the system.

Beware!! Because our solutions in this course are integral, when there appears to be one solution that is all there likely is. As you progress on in your mathematical growth you may encounter deceptive graphs that show two points of intersection if you zoom in when a standard window only shows one. We'll worry about these in later courses – just be aware that this can occur!

Fill in the table with the corresponding Y1 and Y2 values for the given x-values. Use the table to find the solution to the system.

X	Y1	Y2
-3		
-2		
-1		
0		
1		
2		
3		

Solution: _____

Case 3: Graph the following system on your TI-73 and sketch the screen in the space provided.

$$y = 2x^2 - 3x - 1$$
$$y = 2x - 6$$

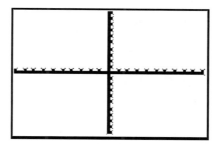

What appears to be happening in the graph of this system?

_____

_____

There are no solutions to this system.

What we need to be careful of in this case is that there may be a solution that does not fall within the standard window.

Try this system:
$$y = 20x^2 - 60x - 200$$
$$y = 23\frac{1}{3}x - 213\frac{1}{3}$$

Can you tell what is happening when you graph these equations in a standard window?

_____

_____

With this particular system the table will work to find the solution but we do have one other option that should be reserved **just for checking**!!

We can set the two equations equal to each other in Solver:

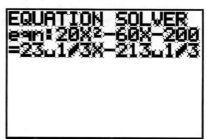

When we solve for x we find that there is a solution at _____ .

Is this the complete solution to the system?

_____

Go back to the homescreen and enter either equation. The value we found in Solver will automatically take x's place as long as we haven't done any other solving or graphing.

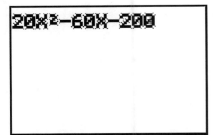

Now put the x and y-values together for the final answer:

_____

Practice: Graph each system on your TI-73 and sketch the screen in the space provided. Use the table to find the solution(s) to each system if they exist.

1. $y = x + 2$

    $y = x^2 - 6x + 8$

    _____

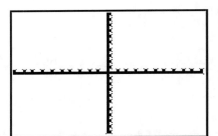

2. $y = 2x - 2$

    $y = -x^2 + 3x + 4$

    _____

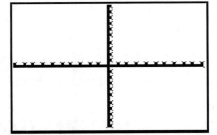

3. $y = -3x + 5$

    $y = 2x^2 + x - 1$

    _____

4. $y = 2x + 3$

         $y = -x^2 + 5x - 6$

         _____

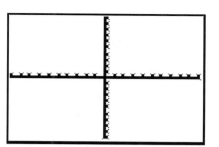

5. $y = \dfrac{1}{2}x^2 - 4x + 8$

         $y = 0$

         _____

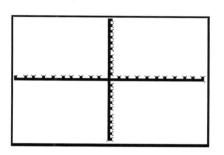

6. $y = -2x^2 + 3x + 2$

         $y = -2x + 5$

         _____

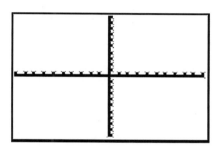

7. $y = x - 3$

         $y = \dfrac{1}{2}x^2 + 3x - 9$

         _____

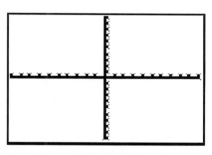

8. $y = x^2 - 11x + 28$

         $y = -5x + 20$

         _____

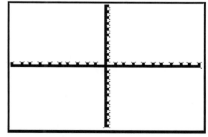

Regents Connection

Solving Systems

Jan '10, #3: Julia went to the movies and bought one jumbo popcorn and two chocolate chip cookies for $5.00. Marvin went to the same movie and bought one jumbo popcorn and four chocolate chip cookies for $6.00. How much does one chocolate chip cookie cost?

    (1) $0.50   (2) $0.75   (3) $1.00   (4) $2.00

_____

Jan '10, #12: Which ordered pair is a solution of the system of equations shown in the graph below?

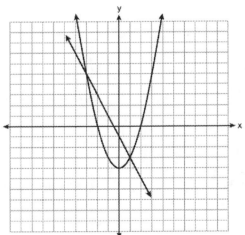

    (1) $(-3,1)$ (2) $(-3,5)$ (3) $(0,-1)$ (4) $(0,-4)$

_____

Aug '09, #20: What is the value of the y-coordinated of the solution to the system of equations $x - 2y = 1$ and $x + 4y = 7$?

    (1) 1   (2) -1 (3) 3   (4) 4

_____

<u>Aug '09, #38</u>: On the grid below, solve the system of equations graphically for x and y.

$$4x - 2y = 10$$
$$y = -2x - 1$$

<u>Jun '09, #25</u>: What is the value of the y-coordinate of the solution to the system of equations $x + 2y = 9$ and $x - y = 3$?

    (1) 6   (2) 2   (3) 3   (4) 5

<u>Jan '09, #22</u>: Which ordered pair is a solution of the system of equations $y = x^2 - x - 20$ and $y = 3x - 15$?

    (1) $(-5, -30)$ (2) $(-1, -18)$ (3) $(0, 5)$ (4) $(5, -1)$

Jun '09, #39: On the set of axes below, solve the following system of equations graphically for all values of x and y.

$$y = x^2 - 6x + 1$$
$$y + 2x = 6$$

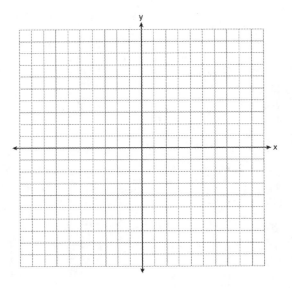

Jan '09, #37: Solve the following system of equations algebraically:

$$3x + 2y = 4$$
$$4x + 3y = 7$$

[Only an algebraic solution can receive full credit.]

Aug '08, #11: Sam and Odel have been selling frozen pizzas for a class fundraiser. Sam has sold half as many pizzas as Odel. Together they have sold a total of 126 pizzas. How many pizzas did Sam sell?

    (1) 21   (2) 42   (3) 63   (4) 84

<u>Aug '08, #12</u>: Which ordered pair is in the solution set of the system of equations $y = -x + 1$ and $y = x^2 + 5x + 6$?

(1) $(-5, -1)$ (2) $(-5, 6)$ (3) $(5, -4)$ (4) $(5, 2)$

<u>Aug '08, #37</u>: The cost of 3 markers and 2 pencils is $1.80. The cost of 4 markers and 6 pencils is $2.90. What is the cost of each item? Include appropriate units in your answer.

<u>Aug '08, #39</u>: On the set of axes below, solve the following system of equations graphically and state the coordinates of all points in the solution set.

$$y = x^2 + 4x - 5$$
$$y = x - 1$$

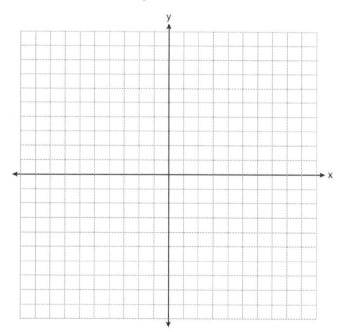

<u>Jun '08, #6</u>: Jack bought 3 slices of cheese pizza, and 4 slices of mushroom pizza for a total cost of $12.50. Grace bought 3 slices of cheese pizza and 2 slices of mushroom pizza for a total cost of $8.50. What is the cost of one slice of mushroom pizza?

(1) $1.50   (2) $2.00   (3) $3.00   (4) $3.50

Jun '08, #10: Which ordered pair is a solution to the system of equations $y = x$ and $y = x^2 - 2$?

(1) $(-2,-2)$ (2) $(-1,1)$ (3) $(0,0)$ (4) $(2,2)$

_____

Sample #38: Solve the following system of equations graphically, on the set of axes below, and state the coordinates of the point(s) in the solution set.

$$y = x^2 - 6x + 5$$
$$2x + 5 = y$$

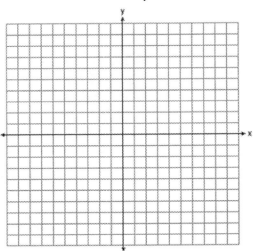

Jun '08, #12: Pam is playing with red and black marbles. The number of red marbles she has is three more than twice the number of black marbles she has. She has 42 marbles in all. How many red marbles does Pam have?

(1) 13   (2) 15   (3) 29   (4) 33

_____

Sample #8: The equations $5x + 2y = 48$ and $3x + 2y = 32$ represent the money collected from school concert ticket sales during two class periods. If x represents the cost for each adult ticket and y represents the cost for each student ticket, what is the cost for each adult ticket?

(1) $20   (2) $10   (3) $8   (4) $4

_____

Jun '10, #12: What is the solution of the system of equations $c + 3d = 8$ and $c = 4d - 6$?

(1) $c = -14, d = -2$ (3) $c = 2, d = 2$
(2) $c = -2, d = 2$ (4) $c = 14, d = -2$

_____

Jun '10, #39: On the set of axes below, solve the following system of equations graphically for all values of x and y.

$$y = -x^2 - 4x + 12$$
$$y = -2x + 4$$

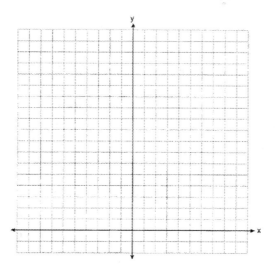

_____

Inequalities

Simple inequalities can be tested with the TI-73.

For example, for which of the following values of x is the given inequality true?

$$\{3,4,5,6\},\ 2x-3<7$$

Store the first value to x, then enter the inequality as it is written. You will find the inequality symbols in the TEXT menu.

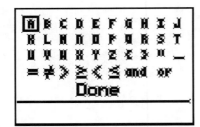 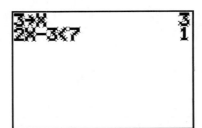

When we test using the TI-73 the answer will be either 1 or 0. If it is a true statement, then the answer will appear as a 1; if it is false the answer will be zero.

So 3 is in the solution set.

Test the remaining members of the set to complete the solution set.

_____

To create a graph of a solution the inequality can be entered in Y_1 and graphed.
Enter $3x-1\geq 5$ in Y_1 and graph in a standard window. Sketch the graph below.

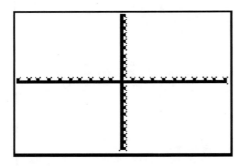

Where does the segment appear to begin?   _____

Does it end?   _____
Use trace and enter the value it appears to begin at. Do you get a y value?

_____

Make a number-line graph of the solution set for the inequality.

Practice:

#1 – 6 Test each set to determine which members of the given set are in the solution set of the inequality.

1. $\{-1,1,3,5\}$ $x+7 \leq 10$

2. $\{3,5,7,9\}$ $x-3 < 8$ _____

3. $\{-3,-2,-1,0,1\}$ $2x+4 > 1$ _____

4. $\{-2,2,4,6\}$ $2x-6 \geq 0$ _____

5. $\{-3,-1,1,3\}$ $3x-7 < -10$ _____

6. $\{-3,-1,1,3\}$ $3x+4 \geq 7$ _____

#7 – 12 Graph the solution set for each inequality.

7. $3x+4 \leq -8$

8. $5x-3 > 7$

9. $4x+3 \geq -5$

10. $x-5 < 7$

11. $x+3 \leq 2$

12. $2x-3 > 5$

_____

Graphing Inequalities

The TI-73 will graph inequalities **and** shade them.

Some things you will need to know:

A. The calculator will not tell whether you should be using a dotted or a solid line. You will need to decide which one to use when you copy your graph onto graph paper:

$$< \text{ or} > \text{ require a dotted line}$$
$$\geq \text{ or } \leq \text{ require a solid line}$$

B. You will need to know which general direction needs to be shaded.

C. This method will not work for vertical lines. Ex: $x = 3$

Let's consider the equation $\qquad y \leq -2x + 5$.

1. Enter the expression $-2x + 5$ in Y_1.

2. Use the left arrow key to move the cursor to the left until the symbol to the left of Y_1 begins to flash.

3. Pressing enter will change the symbol. These are choices to make the appearance of the line different. We will only be concerned with two of these :

  and

The one on the left appears to point down.
We will choose this one when the less than or less than/equal to symbol is used. ($\leq$ or $<$)

The one on the right appears to point up.
We will choose this one when the greater than or greater than/equal to symbol is used. ($\geq$ or $>$).

In the example $\leq$ is used so press ENTER until appears beside Y_1.

5. Press GRAPH .

6. Sketch the screen below: Remember that you need to choose whether the line you sketch must be solid or dotted.

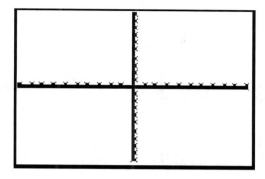

Systems of inequalities are also easily done. Follow the same procedure with your first inequality in Y_1 and the second in Y_2.

The calculator will shade them differently making the solution set (the overlap in the shading) clearly seen. It may be helpful to remember that Y_1 is always shaded vertically and Y_2 is always shaded horizontally.

If your screen becomes very light this is normal. This type of graphing requires more energy from the batteries than most work the calculator is asked to do. You can darken the screen by pressing 2nd and holding down the up arrow until you can see it well again. It will return to normal when you leave the graphing screen.

With the inequality from the first example still in Y_1, enter $y > 3x$ in Y_2.
Graph and sketch the screen below:

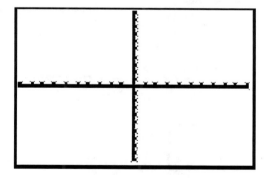

Graphing Inequalities Practice:

Graph and shade each inequality correctly. (Use a standard window.)

1. $y \le 2x + 3$

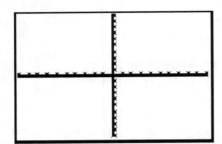

2. $y \ge 2x + 3$

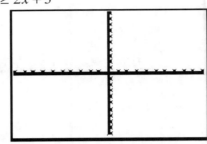

3. $y < 3x$

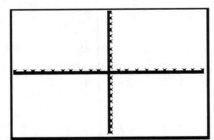

4. $y > 5$

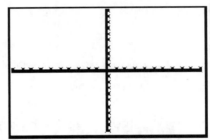

5. $y \le -3x + 5$

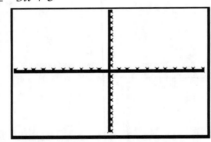

6. $y < -x - 7$

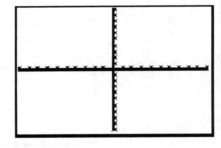

7. $y \ge x - 3$

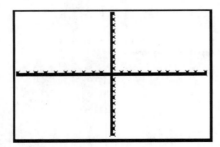

8. $4y > 2x + 8$

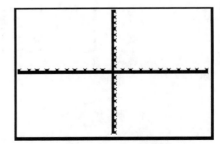

Practice Graphing Systems of Linear Inequalities

For each pair of inequalities
- a. Graph and shade the inequalities on the graphing calculator then sketch the screen in the box given.
- b. Mark the solution set on the sketch with an S.
- c. Give the coordinates of any point **in** the solution set (it is possible that one does not exist).
- d. Give the coordinates of any point **not** in the solution set.

1. $y \le 3x + 4$
   $y > -2x + 1$

   a. & b.

   c. _____

   d. _____

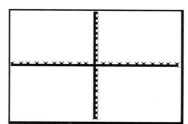

2. $y > -5x - 3$
   $y \le x$

   a. & b.

   c. _____

   d. _____

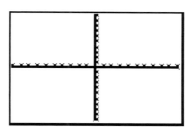

3. $y \le (1/2)x + 1$
   $y < 4x - 3$

   a. & b.

   c. _____

   d. _____

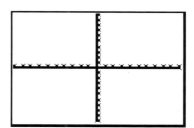

4. $y > 5$
   $y < 6x - 2$

   a. & b.

   c. _____

   d. _____

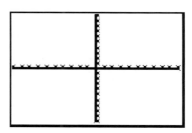

5. $y \geq (2/3)x + 4$
   $y > -5x + 4$

   a. & b.

   c. _____

   d. _____

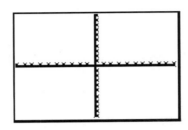

6. $2y < 3x - 7$
   $y \geq 4x - 3$

   a. & b.

   c. _____

   d. _____

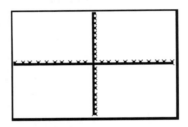

7. $4y > (4/3)x + 8$
   $3y \leq x - 3$

   a. & b.

   c. _____

   d. _____

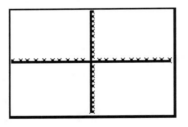

8. $2x - 2y < 6$
   $x + y > 1$

   a. & b.

   c. _____

   d. _____

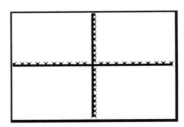

9. $3x < y + 5$
   $x \geq 4y - 12$

   a. & b.

   c. _____

   d. _____

10. $x + 2 > y$
    $-x + 2 < y$

   a. & b.

   c. _____

   d. _____

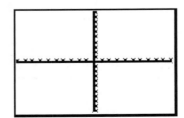

Regents Connection

Inequalities

June '99, #17: If $t^2 < t < \sqrt{t}$, then t could be

(1) $-\dfrac{1}{4}$ (2) 0 (3) $\dfrac{1}{4}$ (4) 4

_____

June '99, #28: A swimmer plans to swim at least 100 laps during a 6-day period. During this period, the swimmer will increase the number of laps completed each day by one lap. What is the least number of laps the swimmer must complete on the first day?

_____

June '01, #18: In the set of positive integers, what is the solution set of the inequality $2x - 3 < 5$?

(1) $\{0,1,2,3\}$ (3) $\{0,1,2,3,4\}$

(2) $\{1,2,3\}$ (4) $\{1,2,3,4\}$

_____

Jan '01, #1: There are 461 students and 20 teachers taking buses on a trip to a museum. Each bus can seat a maximum of 52. What is the least number of buses needed for the trip?

(1) 8 (2) 9 (3) 10 (4) 11

_____

Jan '03, #4: In which list are the numbers in order from least to greatest?

(1) $3.2, \pi, 3\dfrac{1}{3}, \sqrt{3}$ (3) $\sqrt{3}, \pi, 3.2, 3\dfrac{1}{3}$

(2) $\sqrt{3}, 3.2, \pi, 3\dfrac{1}{3}$ (4) $3.2, 3\dfrac{1}{3}, \sqrt{3}, \pi$

_____

<u>Jan '03, #12</u>: Which graph represents the solution set for $2x - 4 \leq 8$ and $x + 5 \geq 7$?

(1)

(2)

(3)

(4)

<u>June '03, #11</u>: Which number is in the solution set of the inequality $5x + 3 > 38$?

(1) 5   (2) 6   (3) 7   (4) 8

<u>June '04, #6</u>: Parking charges at Superior Parking Garage are $5.00 for the first hour and $1.50 for each additional 30 minutes. If Margo has $12.50, what is the maximum amount of time she will be able to park her car at the garage?

(1) $2\frac{1}{2}$ hours   (2) $3\frac{1}{2}$ hours   (3) 6 hours   (4) $6\frac{1}{2}$ hours

<u>Aug '08, #3</u>: Mrs. Smith wrote "Eight less than three times a number is greater than fifteen" on the board. If x represents the number, which inequality is a correct translation of this statement?

(1) $3x - 8 > 15$ (3) $8 - 3x > 15$

(2) $3x - 8 < 15$ (4) $8 - 3x < 15$

<u>Jan '10, #5</u>: Roger is having a picnic for 78 guests. He plans to serve each guest at least one hot dog. If each package, p, contains eight hot dogs, which inequality could be used to determine how many packages of hot dogs Roger will need to buy?

(1) $p \geq 78$ (2) $8p \geq 78$ (3) $8 + p \geq 78$ (4) $78 - p \geq 8$

<u>Jan '10, #23</u>: Which ordered pair is in the solution set of the following system of linear inequalities?

$$y < 2x + 2$$
$$y \geq -x - 1$$

(1) $(0,3)$ (2) $(2,0)$ (3) $(-1,0)$ (4) $(-1,-4)$

_____

<u>Jan '10, #38</u>: Graph the solution set for the inequality $4x - 3y > 9$ on the set of axes below. Determine if the point $(1,-3)$ is in the solution set. Justify your answer.

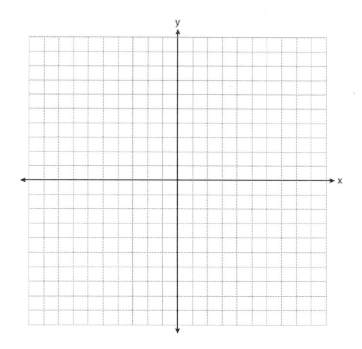

_____

<u>Aug '09, #4</u>: An online music club has a one-time registration fee of $\$13.95$ and charges $\$0.49$ to buy each song. If Emma has $\$50.00$ to join the club and buy songs, what is the maximum number of songs she can buy?

(1) 73   (2) 74   (3) 130   (4) 131

_____

Aug '09, #13: Which value of x is in the solution set of the inequality $-2(x-5)<4$?

(1) 0 (2) 2 (3) 3 (4) 5

Jun '09, #6: The sign shown below is posted in front of a roller coaster fide at the Wadsworth County Fairgrounds.

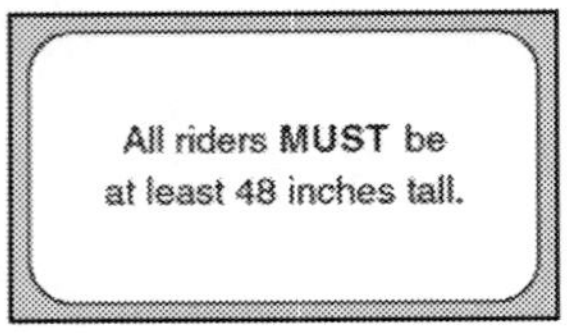
All riders **MUST** be
at least 48 inches tall.

If h represents the height of a rider in inches, what is a correct translation of the statement on this sign?

(1) $h<48$ (2) $h>48$ (3) $h\leq 48$ (4) $h\geq 48$

Jun '09, #14: Which value of x is in the solution set of $\frac{4}{3}x+5<17$?

(1) 8 (2) 9 (3) 12 (4) 16

Jun '09, #20: Which graph represents the solution of $3y-9\leq 6x$?

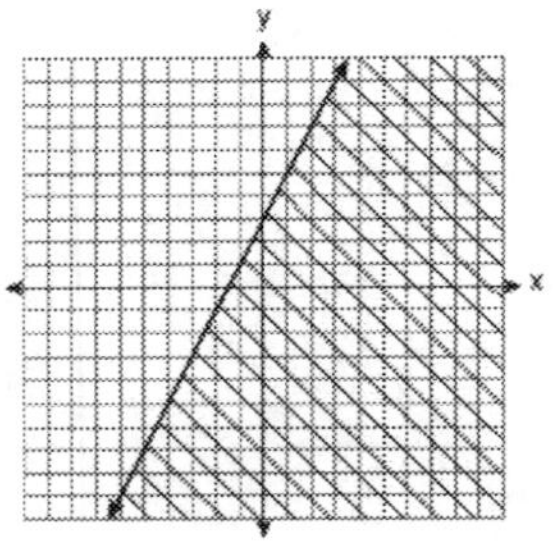
y
x

(1)

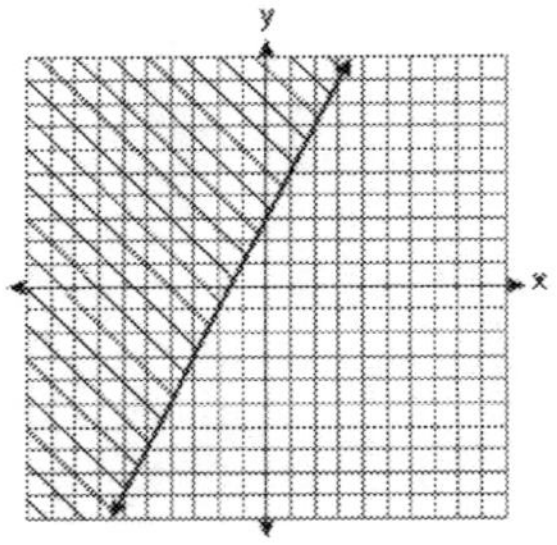
y
x

(3)

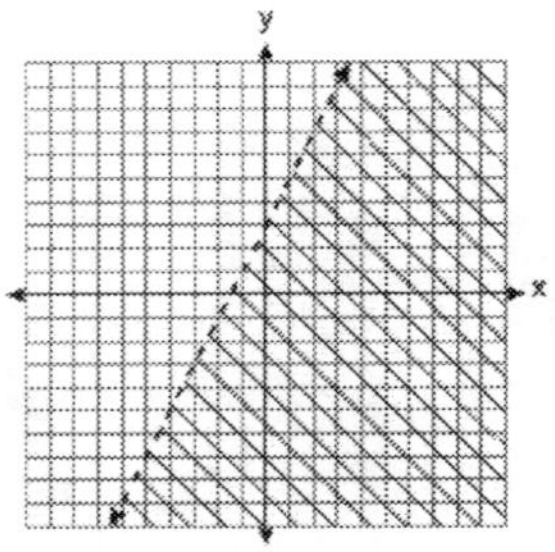
y
x

(2)

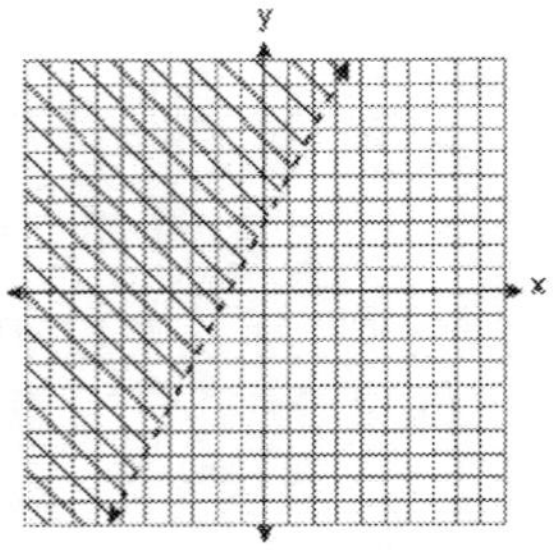
y
x

(4)

<u>Aug '08, #5:</u> Which value of x is in the solution set of the inequality $-4x + 2 > 10$?

(1) -2 (2) 2 (3) 3 (4) -4

_____

<u>Jan '09, #4:</u> Tamara has a cell phone plan that charges $0.07 per minute plus a monthly fee of $19.00. She budgets $29.50 per month for total cell phone expenses without taxes. What is the maximum number of minutes Tamara could use her phone each month in order to stay within her budget?

(1) 150 (2) 271 (3) 421 (4) 692

_____

<u>Jan '09, #38:</u> On the set of axes below, graph the following system of inequalities and state the coordinates of a point in the solution set.

$$2x - y \geq 6$$
$$x > 2$$

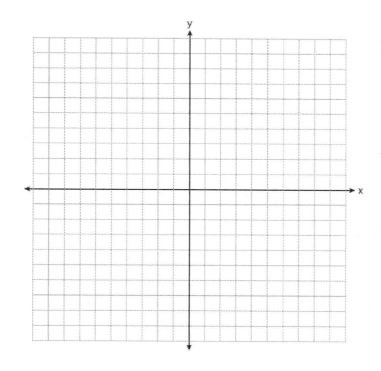

Aug '08, #25: Which ordered pair is in the solution set of the following system of inequalities?

$$y < \frac{1}{2}x + 4$$
$$y \geq -x + 1$$

(1) $(-5,3)$ (2) $(0,4)$ (3) $(3,-5)$ (4) $(4,0)$

____

Jun '08, #21: Students in a ninth grade class measured their heights, h, in centimeters. The height of the shortest student was $155cm$, and the height of the tallest student was $190cm$. Which inequality represents the range of heights?

(1) $155 < h < 190$
(2) $155 \leq h \leq 190$
(3) $h \geq 155$ or $h \leq 190$
(4) $h > 155$ or $h < 190$

____

Jun '08, #34: Peter begins his kindergarten year able to spell 10 words. He is going to learn to spell 2 new words every day. Write an inequality that can be used to determine how many days, d, it takes Peter to be able to spell at least 75 words.

____

Use this inequality to determine the minimum number of whole days it will take for him to be able to spell at least 75 words.

____

Sample #15: An electronics store sells DVD players and cordless telephones. The store makes a $\$75$ profit on the sale of each DVD player (d) and a $\$30$ profit on the sale of each cordless telephone (c). The store wants to make a profit of at least $\$255.00$ from its sales of DVD players and cordless phones. Which inequality describes this situation?

(1) $75d + 30c < 255$
(2) $75d + 30c \leq 255$
(3) $75d + 30c > 255$
(4) $75d + 30c \geq 255$

____

Sample #24: Which value of x is in the solution set of the inequality $-2x + 5 > 17$?

(1) -8 (2) -6 (3) -4 (4) 12

____

Sample #35: A prom ticket at Smith High School is $\$120$. Tom is going to save money for the ticket by walking his neighbor's dog for $\$15$ per week. If Tom has saved $\$22$, what is the minimum number of weeks Tom must walk the dog to earn enough to pay for the prom ticket?

____

<u>Sample #20</u>: Which inequality is represented by the graph below?

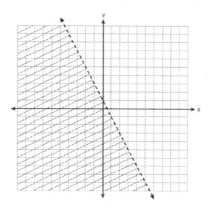

(1) $y < 2x + 1$ (3) $y < \dfrac{1}{2}x + 1$

(2) $y < -2x + 1$ (4) $y < -\dfrac{1}{2}x + 1$

_____

<u>Jun '10, #10</u>: Which ordered pair is in the solution set of the system of linear inequalities graphed below?

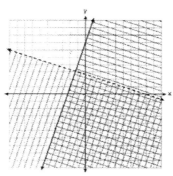

(1) $(1, -4)$ (2) $(-5, 7)$ (3) $(5, 3)$ (4) $(-7, -2)$

_____

<u>Jun '10, #28</u>: Which quadrant will be completely shaded in the graph of the inequality $y \le 2x$?

(1) Quadrant I (3) Quadrant III
(2) Quadrant II (4) Quadrant IV

_____

<u>Jun '10, #34</u>: Given: $A = \{18, 6, -3, -12\}$

Determine all elements of set A that are in the solution of the inequality $\dfrac{2}{3}x + 3 < -2x - 7$.

_____

Pythagorean Theorem

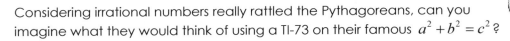

Considering irrational numbers really rattled the Pythagoreans, can you imagine what they would think of using a TI-73 on their famous $a^2 + b^2 = c^2$?

The method we will use will work on most formulas but is generally more work than doing the problem on paper or making your substitutions first and only using one unknown.

It does work very well if you have several of the same type of problem.

Just remember that a and b are the _____ , and c is the

_____ even if they are given different names in the problem.

First enter the formula in SOLVER:

 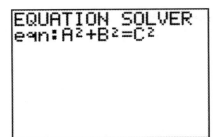

When you press ENTER, all three variables should appear.

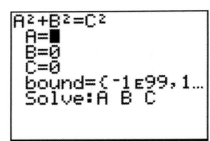

You should know two of the three values. Enter these, then choose the variable you need to find after "Solve:".

Let's try it.

In right triangle ABC with $C = 90°$, $AB = 12$, and $BC = 7$, find AC.

(Draw the triangle first!)

Practice:

Find the missing value for each known pair. Assume that $\angle C$ is the right angle in each triangle. (Round decimals to the nearest hundredth.)

A. a=11, b=15, c=_____

B. a=6, b=10, c=_____

C. a=1, b=1, c=_____

D. a=3, b=8, c=_____

E. a=_____, b=11, c=15

F. a=_____, b=12, c=13

G. a=_____, b=7, c=16

H. a=11, b=_____, c=20

I. a=25, b=30, c=_____

J. a=25, b=_____, c=40

K. a=81, b=99, c=_____

L. a=64, b=_____, c=100

M. a=29, b=50, c=_____

N. a=_____, b=3, c=7

Regents Connection

Pythagorean Theorem

Aug '09, #6: Nancy's rectangular garden is represented in the diagram below.

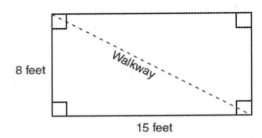

If a diagonal walkway crosses her garden, what is its length in feet?

(1) 17   (2) 22   (3) $\sqrt{161}$ (4) $\sqrt{529}$

_____

Jun '09, #9: What is the value of x, in inches, in the right triangle below?

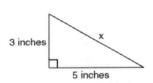

(1) $\sqrt{15}$ (2) 8   (3) $\sqrt{34}$ (4) 4

_____

Aug '08, #9: The length of the hypotenuse of a right triangle is 34 inches and the length of one of its legs is 16 inches. What is the length, in inches, of the other leg of this right triangle?

(1) 16   (2) 18   (3) 25   (4) 30

_____

<u>Jun '08, #25</u>: Don placed a ladder against the side of his house as shown in the diagram below.

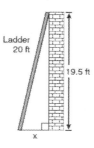

Ladder
20 ft

19.5 ft

x

Which equation could be used to find the distance, x, from the foot of the ladder to the base of the house?

(1) $x = 20 - 19.5$

(3) $x = \sqrt{20^2 - 19.5^2}$

(2) $x = 20^2 - 19.5^2$

(4) $x = \sqrt{20^2 + 19.5^2}$

<u>Sample #11</u>: Tanya runs diagonally across a rectangular field that has a length of 40 yards and a width of 30 yards, as shown in the diagram below.

x

40 yards

30 yards

What is the length of the diagonal, in yards, that Tanya runs?

(1) 50   (2) 60   (3) 70   (4) 80

SOH-CAH-TOA

Sine, cosine, and tangent are _____ used to represent relationships between

the sides of a _____ using the _____ angles

of the triangle.

Sine= $\dfrac{opposite}{hypotenuse}$ Cosine= $\dfrac{adjacent}{hypotenuse}$ Tangent= $\dfrac{opposite}{adjacent}$

SOH   CAH   TOA

When the TI-73 has been reset it will be in _____ mode.

```
              Sci
Float  0123456789
Degree Radian
Aub/c b/c
Autosimp Mansimp
```

This is the mode you will need for these ratios. Be aware that most other calculators are in

_____ mode when they are reset and will need to be changed!!

The trigonometry functions are found be pressing [2ND] [DRAW]

```
TRIG ANGLE
1:sin(
2:sin⁻¹(
3:cos(
4:cos⁻¹(
5:tan(
6:tan⁻¹(
```

The adjacent side is: _____

The opposite side is: _____

The hypotenuse is: _____

The angle is measured in: _____

In each right triangle trigonometry problem, you will be given two sides and an angle. Two will be known values, the third you will need to solve for.

The ratios can be done on the home screen if you are familiar with them or they can be done in SOLVER:

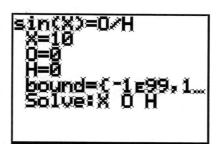

Enter the parts you know and solve for the third variable.

Be sure to use the parentheses correctly. The calculator automatically enters the beginning of the set of parentheses when you choose the trigonometry function. You must end them after the part of the equation that represents the degrees.

Also **sketch a diagram** that represents the problem first so that you are using the correct function.

    a. In each diagram below circle the three parts of the triangle you are given.
        (Assume each triangle is a right triangle.)
    b. Write the trigonometry function you would need to solve. **You do not need to find the missing value!

1.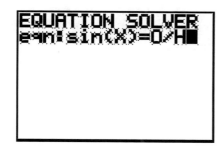

2.

3.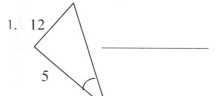

4.

5.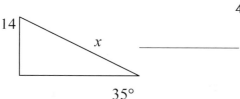

6.

Hints:

To elevate means to move _____ .
An angle of elevation is an angle which begins horizontally and moves up.

To depress or descend means to move _____ .
An angle of depression or of descent begins horizontally and moves down.

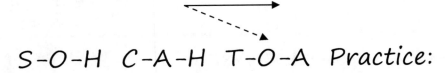

S-O-H C-A-H T-O-A Practice:

Find the missing part of each right triangle below. Round to the nearest thousandth.

1.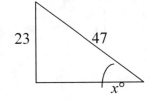

    23   47

    $x°$

    x = _____

2.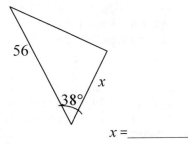

    56

    x

    38°

    x = _____

3.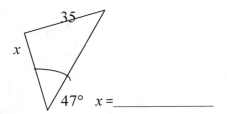

    35

    x

    47°   x = _____

4.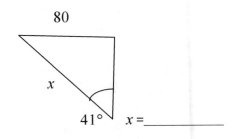

    x

    17

    20°

    x = _____

5.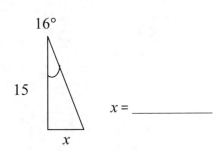

    16°

    15

    x

    x = _____

6.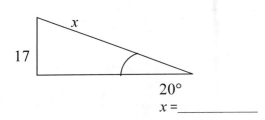

    80

    x

    41°   x = _____

Tackling Trigonometric Word Problems

Be sure to **sketch a diagram** that represents the problem first so that you are using the correct function! Show all work or explain how you found your answer.

A. The tailgate of a truck is 2 feet above the ground. The incline of a ramp used for loading Kyle's snowmobile on the truck is 11°. Find to the nearest tenth of a foot, the length of the ramp.

_____

B. Adam is snowboarding down a steep hill. Jordan is watching from the bottom of the hill and measures the angle of inclination as 65°. If it takes Adam 2 minutes to descend the hill at an average speed of 35 mph, how high vertically up the hill did Adam start? (In other words, what is the relative altitude of his starting point?)

_____

C. Josh is four-wheeling with friends and is embarrassed when he cannot climb a particular hill. He notices that he always seems to get stuck when hills have a certain steepness. In order to avoid future embarrassment he returns later to measure the hill. From the base of the hill to the point he got stuck is 50 feet. Walking parallel to the hill, he estimates that the horizontal distance is 25 feet. What angle of inclination should he avoid with his four-wheeler? (At least until he saves up to buy one with a more powerful motor!)

_____

D. Rachel is babysitting two children who have a cranky neighbor. They go out to fly kites, but Rachel must be sure that the kites do not fly over the neighbor's property. Under current wind conditions, the kites are flying at a $50°$ angle and the ideal location is 100 feet from the neighbor's property. At what length should Rachel limit the kites' string?

_____

E. Alex is sitting in his tree stand when he sights an eight-point buck. He wants to wait until the deer is 100 yards away. He knows his tree stand is 12 feet up in the tree. What angle of depression in his line of vision should he be waiting to fire at?

_____

F. You are trying to find how wide Black River is. You are standing on one side, your friend is on the other. You fly a kite so that it crosses over to the other side. When your friend says that the kite is directly overhead, you measure the angle of elevation as $65°$ and the kite string has been let out to 220 feet. How wide is the river at this point?

_____

Regents Connection

Trigonometry

Jan '10, #8: Which equation shows a correct trigonometric ratio for angle A in the right triangle below?

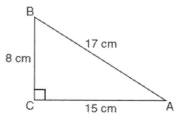

(1) $\sin A = \dfrac{15}{17}$ (2) $\tan A = \dfrac{8}{17}$ (3) $\cos A = \dfrac{15}{17}$ (4) $\tan A = \dfrac{15}{8}$

_____

Jan '10, #32: In right triangle ABC, $AB = 20$, $AC = 12$, $BC = 16$, and $m\angle C = 90$. Find, to the nearest degree, the measure of $\angle A$.

_____

Aug '09, #14: A tree casts a 25-foot shadow on a sunny day, as shown in the diagram below.

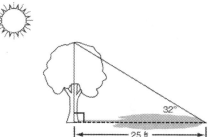

If the angle of elevation from the tip of the shadow to the top of the tree is $32°$, what is the height of the tree to the nearest tenth of a foot?

     (1) 13.2   (2) 15.6   (3) 21.2   (4) 40.0

_____

<u>Jun '09, #37</u>: A stake is to be driven into the ground away from the base of a 50-foot pole, as shown in the diagram below. A wire from the stake on the ground to the top of the pole is to be installed at an angle of elevation of 52°.

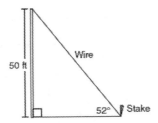

How far away from the base of the pole should the stake be driven in, to the nearest foot?

_____

What will be the length of the wire from the stake to the top of the pole, to the nearest foot?

_____

<u>Jan '09, #12</u>: In the right triangle shown in the diagram below, what is the value of x to the nearest whole number?

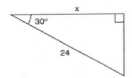

(1) 12   (2) 14   (3) 21   (4) 28

_____

<u>Jan '09, #19</u>: The diagram below shows right triangle UPC.

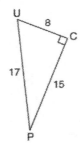

Which ratio represents the sine of $\angle U$?

(1) $\dfrac{15}{8}$ (2) $\dfrac{15}{17}$ (3) $\dfrac{8}{15}$ (4) $\dfrac{8}{17}$

_____

<u>Aug '08, #24</u>: Which expression could be used to find the measure of one acute angle in the right triangle shown below?

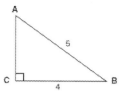

(1) $\sin A = \dfrac{4}{5}$

(2) $\tan A = \dfrac{5}{4}$

(3) $\cos B = \dfrac{5}{4}$

(4) $\tan B = \dfrac{4}{5}$

<u>Aug '08, #29</u>: In the diagram of $\triangle ABC$ shown below, $BC = 10$ and $AB = 16$.

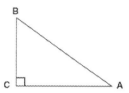

To the nearest tenth of a degree, what is the measure of the largest acute angle in the triangle?

(1) 32.0   (2) 38.7   (3) 51.3   (4) 90.0

<u>Jun '08, #16</u>: The center pole of a tent is 8 feet long, and a side of the tent is 12 feet long as shown in the diagram below.

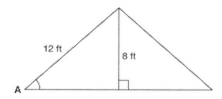

If a right angle is formed where the center pole meets the ground, what is the measure of angle A to the nearest degree?

(1) 34   (2) 42   (3) 48   (4) 56

Sample #21: In triangle MCT, the measure of $\angle T = 09°$ m $MC = 85cm$, $CT = 84cm$, and $TM = 13cm$. Which ratio represents the sine of $\angle C$?

(1) $\dfrac{13}{85}$ (2) $\dfrac{84}{85}$ (3) $\dfrac{13}{84}$ (4) $\dfrac{84}{13}$

Jun '10, #9: In $\triangle ABC$, the measure of $\angle B = 90°$, $AC = 50$, $AB = 48$, and $BC = 14$. Which ratio represents the tangent of $\angle A$?

(1) $\dfrac{14}{50}$ (2) $\dfrac{14}{48}$ (3) $\dfrac{48}{50}$ (4) $\dfrac{48}{14}$

Jun '10, #33: A communications company is building a 30-foot antenna to carry cell phone transmissions. As shown in the diagram below, a 50-foot wire from the top of the antenna to the ground is used to stabilize the antenna.

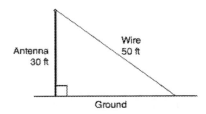

Find, to the nearest degree, the measure of the angle that the wire makes with the ground.

The Counting Principle

When calculating probabilities, we must first find how many possible outcomes there are.

Sometimes this will be very obvious. Other times we will need to do some calculating.

When we are looking at possible numbers of combinations of different types of objects we

can use_____.

The counting principle says that the number of possibilities is the _____ of

the number of objects in each set.

Example: A school's lunch menu allows students to choose one item from each of the
following lists:

Beverage:	Sandwich:	Soup:	Dessert:
Milk	Peanut Butter	Tomato	Fruit
Chocolate milk	Tuna	Vegetable	Cookie
Juice	Turkey		Ice Cream

Because there are 3 beverages, 3 sandwiches, 2 soups, and 3 desserts, there are

$3 \times 3 \times 2 \times 3 =$ _____ possible menu combinations.

***This assumes that a student must take one choice from each group.**

Suppose a student may choose not to have a selection from each list. What if the school
policy says that they may not choose only a beverage, only a dessert, or only a beverage
and dessert.
Now the possible combinations are:

_____ _____ _____ _____

_____ _____ _____

_____ _____ _____

_____ _____ _____

_____ _____ _____

_____ _____ _____

_____ _____

_____ _____

_____ _____

_____ _____

_____ _____

Use the counting principle on each combination and find the sum of all of these combinations.

How many students could eat lunch and no two of them have the same combination of foods?

_____

Practice:

1. If Sally has 4 shirts, 2 skirts, and 3 sweaters that are color coordinated, how many different outfits can she put together assuming that she chooses one item from each group?

    _____

2. Mary is wallpapering her bedroom. She has found 5 patterns that she likes. Each pattern has 4 coordinating borders and 9 choices for coordinating paint for the trim. How many combinations does she have to choose from?

    _____

3. In Jim's senior year he can choose from 3 English courses, 2 social studies electives, 3 math courses, 2 science courses, and he has room in his schedule for an elective of his choice from a list of 10. How many possible combinations of courses could he take? (Assume he must take one English, one math, one social studies, and one science course, and he will take another course as an elective.)

    _____

4. An ice cream shop claims to be able to serve 1000 different sundaes. They offer the following choices:

Ice Cream Flavors:	Toppings:	Extras (choose 2):
Vanilla	Hot Fudge	Chocolate Sprinkles
Chocolate	Chocolate	Rainbow Sprinkles
Strawberry	Caramel	Whipped Cream
Orange Sherbet	Marshmallow	Peanuts
Cookie Dough	Strawberry	Walnuts
Mint Chocolate Chip		Maraschino Cherry

    Are they being honest? Explain.

    _____

    _____

    _____

Probability:
Compound Events

There are several cases that must be considered when we go beyond simple probability.

When more than one "event" occurs, sometimes the outcome of that event will effect the probability of the "event" paired with it and sometimes it won't.

Independent Events:

When the two (or more) events will have no effect on each other they are considered

_____.

Ex: Rolling a die, then flipping a coin.

One way to calculate the probability would be to make a tree diagram:

You could also make a list of all the possible outcomes:

We can also calculate the number of outcomes: (Use the counting principle)

Dependent Events:

If the events are not exclusive or in any way influence the outcome of other events, they are called_____.

Example 1: At the awards assembly 10 students are eligible for 3 awards. What is the probability that a particular one of the 10 will receive an award?

What information do you need before you can calculate the probability?

_____

_____

If one student can receive more than one award, the probability is different than if a student can only receive one award. What is the number of possibilities in each case?

_____

And vs. Or:

Which would you expect to be higher, the probability of rolling a 3 *and* a coin landing on heads, or the probability of rolling a 3 *or* a coin landing on heads?

_____

Remember that probabilities are _____

Which produces a smaller number, adding two numbers ≤ 1 or multiplying two numbers ≤ 1?

_____

If you are looking at the probability that both events have favorable outcomes, multiply the probabilities of the individual events.
If you are looking at the probability that one or the other of two events will have a favorable outcome, add the probabilities but subtract out any overlapping possibilities.

With or Without Replacement:

It matters if an object is returned to the set being drawn from if there is a favorable outcome on the first trial.

In the previous example, it mattered if a student was returned to the "pool" of possible award winners.

When replacing the original object, that probabilities are not changed.

Example: What is the probability of drawing a black card three times in a row if the card drawn *is replaced* each time? (Black *and* Black *and* Black)

_____

When the first trial results in a favorable outcome and the object is not returned to the set of possible results, there are two possibilities:
    1. Are you looking for another outcome from the same set as the first one,
    2. Or, is a favorable outcome for the second trial different than it was for the first?

In the first case, you will need to subtract one from both the numerator and the denominator of your second probability before multiplying.
In the second case, you will need to subtract only from the denominator.

Example: What is the probability of drawing a black queen, then drawing any black card *without replacement*? (Black Queen *and* Black)

_____

Example: What is the probability of drawing a black queen, then drawing a red card *without replacement*? (Black Queen *and* Red)

_____

Practice:

1. What is the probability of a coin landing heads and a die landing on an even number?

    _____

2. What is the probability of a die landing on a prime number and drawing a heart from a standard deck?

    _____

3. What is the probability that a coin will land on tails, or a die will land on a multiple of 3?
    (Remember to subtract out those cases where both are occurring or you will be counting them twice.)

    _____

4. If a package of m&m's contains 15 blue, 20 green, and 13 red m&m's, what is the probability of drawing one of each when picking them out of the package one at a time without looking?

    _____

    What is the probability of getting all three m&m's the same color?

    _____

Combinations, Permutations, and Factorials

Combinations are: _____ $_nC_r$

_____

Permutations are:

_____ $_nP_r$

_____

Factorial notation is used for: _____ !

_____

All of these can be performed on the graphing calculator by pressing

MATH then choosing the PRB (probability) menu.

The factorial _notation_ is important to know. When using the factorial option you must input the number first, then go to the probability menu and choose #5.

Practice with these:

a. 3! = _____ b. 5! = _____ c. 7! = _____ d. 9! = _____

How do you know when to use $_nC_r$ and when to use $_nP_r$?

_____

_____

_____

When using the $_nC_r$ or $_nP_r$:
1. Input "n" (the number of possible choices).
2. Go to the probability menu and select #2 or 3.
3. Input "r" (how many out of the possible choices you will be selecting).

Practice:

a. $_5C_5 = $ _____ b. $_3C_2 = $ _____ c. $_7C_3 = $ _____ d. $_8C_3 = $ _____

e. $_6C_4 = $ _____ f. $_{10}C_2 = $ _____ g. $_{20}C_{11} = $ _____ h. $_{25}C_{20} = $ _____

i. $_5P_5 = $ _____ j. $_3P_2 = $ _____ k. $_6P_1 = $ _____ l. $_8P_3 = $ _____

m. $_6P_4 = $ _____ n. $_{10}P_2 = $ _____

o. $_{20}P_{11} = $ _____ p. $_{25}P_{20} = $ _____

q. Suppose the bookstore has 10 new books in. They will choose 5 of these to display in the front window. How many combinations of 5 books are possible?

_____

r. A special committee is being set up in the US Senate. 10 senators will be chosen at random in the interest of fairness. How many combinations of senators are possible in this committee?

_____

s. Your grandmother has ordered a dozen tulip bulbs and asks you to plant them around her wishing well. Each bulb is a different color and the wishing well has a square base. The bulbs are not labeled so you randomly plant them evenly around the base of the well with none on the corners. How many color arrangements are possible on any one side of the well?

_____

t. One lottery game asks you to choose 4 numbers $0-99$. You win regardless of the order you list your numbers.
Another lottery game asks you to list 5 numbers $0-25$, but you only win if they are in the exact order the winning numbers are chosen. In which game is your chance of winning better? Explain using the probabilities for each game.

_____

_____

_____

Regents Connection
Probability

Jan '10 #2: A bag contains eight green marbles, five white marbles, and two red marbles. What is the probability of drawing a red marble from the bag?

(1) $\dfrac{1}{15}$ (2) $\dfrac{2}{15}$ (3) $\dfrac{2}{13}$ (4) $\dfrac{13}{15}$

_____

Jan '10, #33: Jon is buying tickets for himself for two concerts. For the jazz concert, 4 tickets are available in the front row, and 32 tickets are available in the other rows. For the orchestra concert, 3 tickets are available in the front row, and 23 tickets are available in the other rows. Jon is randomly assigned one ticket for each concert.

Determine the concert for which he is more likely to get a front-row ticket. Justify your answer.

_____

Jan '10, #37: A password consists of three digits, 0 through 9, followed by three letters from an alphabet having 26 letters. If repetition of digits is allowed, but repetition of letters is not allowed, determine the number of different passwords that can be made.

_____

If repetition is not allowed for digits or letters, determine how many fewer different passwords can be made.

_____

Aug '09, #5: The local ice cream stand offers three flavors of soft-serve ice cream: vanilla, chocolate, and strawberry; two types of cone: sugar and wafer; and three toppings: sprinkles, nuts, and cookie crumbs. If Dawn does not order vanilla ice cream, how many different choices can she make that have one flavor of ice cream, one type of cone, and one topping?

(1) 7   (2) 8   (3) 12   (4) 18

_____

<u>Aug '09, #7</u>: The spinner below is divided into eight equal regions and is spun once. What is the probability of not getting red?

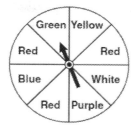

(1) $\dfrac{3}{5}$ (2) $\dfrac{3}{8}$ (3) $\dfrac{5}{8}$ (4) $\dfrac{7}{8}$

<u>Aug '09, #33</u>: Clayton has three fair coins. Find the probability that he gets two tails and one head when he flips the three coins.

<u>Jun '09, #8</u>: Students in Ms. Nazzeer's mathematics class tossed a six-sided number cube whose faces are numbered 1 to 6. The results are recorded in the table below.

Result	Frequency
1	3
2	6
3	4
4	6
5	4
6	7

Based on these data, what is the empirical probability of tossing a 4?

(1) $\dfrac{8}{30}$ (2) $\dfrac{6}{30}$ (3) $\dfrac{5}{30}$ (4) $\dfrac{1}{30}$

<u>Jun '09, #31</u>: Determine how many three-letter arrangements are possible with the letters $A, N, G, L,$ and E if no letter may be repeated.

<u>Jun '09, #33</u>: Some books are laid on a desk. Two are English, three are mathematics, one is French, and four are social studies. Theresa selects an English book and Isabelle then selects a social studies book. Both girls take their selections to the Library to read. If Truman then selects a book at random, what is the probability that he selects an English book?

_____

<u>Jan '09, #3</u>: The faces of a cube are numbered from 1 to 6. If the cube is rolled once, which outcome is least likely to occur?

    (1) rolling an odd number
    (2) rolling an even number
    (3) rolling a number less than 6
    (4) rolling a number greater than 4

_____

<u>Jan '09, #28</u>: Keisha is playing a game using a wheel divided into eight equal sectors, as shown in the diagram below. Each time the spinner lands on orange, she will win a prize.

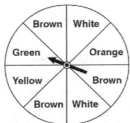

If Keisha spins this wheel twice, what is the probability she will win a prize on both spins?

  (1) $\dfrac{1}{64}$ (2) $\dfrac{1}{56}$ (3) $\dfrac{1}{16}$ (4) $\dfrac{1}{4}$

_____

A restaurant sells kids' meals consisting of one main course, one side dish, and one drink, as shown in the table below.

Kids' Meal Choices

Main Course	Side Dish	Drink
hamburger	French fries	milk
chicken nuggets	applesauce	juice
turkey sandwich		soda

Draw a tree diagram or list the sample space showing all possible kids' meals. How many different kids' meals can a person order?

Jose does not drink juice. Determine the number of different kids' meals that do not include juice.

Jose's sister will eat only chicken nuggets for her main course. Determine the number of different kids' meals that include chicken nuggets.

Aug '08, #16: John is going to line up his four golf trophies on a shelf in his bedroom. How many different possible arrangements can he make?

(1) 24   (2) 16   (3) 10   (4) 4

Aug '08, #30: The faces of a cube are numbered from 1 to 6. If the cube is tossed once, what is the probability that a prime number or a number divisible by 2 is obtained?

(1) $\dfrac{6}{6}$ (2) $\dfrac{5}{6}$ (3) $\dfrac{4}{6}$ (4) $\dfrac{1}{6}$

Aug '08, #32: Brianna is using the two spinners shown below to play her new board game. She spins the arrow on each spinner once. Brianna uses the first spinner to determine how many spaces to move. She uses the second spinner to determine whether her move from the first spinner will be forward or backward.

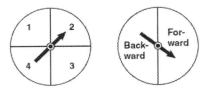

Find the probability that Brianna will move fewer than four spaces and backward.

Jun '08, #2: A spinner is divided into eight equal regions as shown in the diagram below?

Which event is most likely to occur in one spin?

   (1) The arrow will land in a green or white area.
   (2) The arrow will land in a green or black area.
   (3) The arrow will land in a yellow or black area.
   (4) The arrow will land in a yellow or green area.

Jun '08, #8: The bowling team at Lincoln High School must choose a president, vice president, and secretary. If the team has 10 members, which expression could be used to determine the number of ways the officers could be chosen?

   (1) $_3P_{10}$ (2) $_7P_3$ (3) $_{10}P_3$ (4) $_{10}P_7$

Sample #2: Throughout history, many people have contributed to the development of mathematics. These mathematicians include Pythagoras, Euclid, Hypatia, Euler, Einstein, Agnesi, Fibonacci, and Pascal. What is the probability that a mathematician's name selected at random from those listed will start with either the letter E or the letter A?

   (1) $\dfrac{2}{8}$ (2) $\dfrac{3}{8}$ (3) $\dfrac{4}{8}$ (4) $\dfrac{6}{8}$

Sample #36: Mr. Lamb has three children: two girls (Sue and Karen) and one boy (David). After each meal, one child is chosen at random to wash dishes.
If the same child can be chosen for both lunch and dinner, construct a tree diagram or list a sample space of all the possible outcomes of who will wash dishes after lunch and dinner on Saturday.

Determine the probability that one boy and one girl will wash dishes after lunch and dinner on Saturday.

Jun '10, #2: How many different sandwiches consisting of one type of cheese, one condiment, and one bread choice can be prepared from five types of cheese, two condiments, and three bread choices?

    (1) 10   (2) 13   (3) 15   (4) 30

Jun '10, #6: Three high school juniors, Reese, Matthew, and Chris, are running for student council president. A survey is taken a week before the election asking 40 students which candidate they will vote for in the election. The results are shown in the table below.

Candidate's Name	Number of Students Supporting Candidate
Reese	15
Matthew	13
Chris	12

Based on the table, what is the probability that a student will vote for Reese?

    (1) $\dfrac{1}{3}$ (2) $\dfrac{3}{5}$ (3) $\dfrac{3}{8}$ (4) $\dfrac{5}{8}$

Jun '10, #26: How many different three-letter arrangements can be formed using the letters in the word _ABSOLUTE_ if each letter is used only once?

    (1) 56   (2) 112   (3) 168   (4) 336

Appendix A

Sending and Receiving

Linking your calculator with another calculator or computer allows you so update the operating system and share applications, programs, and lists.

To connect to another calculator:

1. Use a unit-to-unit cable to connect the two calculators. The port is located cn the bottom end of the calculator. Be sure they are firmly connected.

2. Press APPS

3. A screen similar to the one at the right should appear. You may have different Applications listed but the first one should always be 1:Link.

4. One calculator will choose to RECEIVE. This calculator should be ready first and read "waiting". Press ENTER at the screen shown. (Note: If you change your mind after you have chosen to receive you can stop the calculator by holding down the ON key.

5. The other calculator should now choose to SEND. Choose what type of item you wish to send by pressing ENTER or the number of the choice. (Note: Sending ALL takes a long time!)

6. You will now have the opportunity to choose more specifically what to send then you should TRANSMIT. You can tell that an item has been selected if it has a block shape in front of it. In the screen at the right AREAFORM and GEOBOARD have been selected. The cursor is on MATRICES but it has not been selected.

7. Wait until both calculators read "DONE" before disconnecting them!

To connect to a computer:

1. You will need TI Connect installed on your computer and a TI-Graph Link cable. If your calculator did not come with one of these cables they can be purchased or borrowed. The TI Connect software can be downloaded free from education.ti.com.

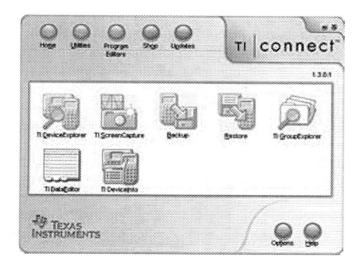

2. TI Connect can back-up your own files or allow you to download files from the Internet to a file on your computer, and then transfer these to your calculator. This may come in handy if you have some Applications or programs you especially like but your teacher has said everything must be cleared before you use your calculator on a test.

3. With TI Connect installed you should be able to right-click on the file and choose "Send to TI Device" to transfer it to the calculator.

4. You can also use "Screen Capture" to use your current screen as clipart in a document on your computer. The pictures on the previous page were made on a TI-73 calculator and captured with TI Connect.

Appendix B

Managing the Memory

Have you tried to install a new application only to find that you don't have space?

Do you know how much space is available on your calculator? Let's find out.

Press then to access the Memory.

Choose 3:Check APPs...

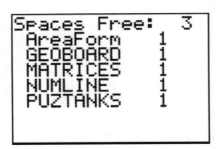

You should see all of your applications listed as well as how many spaces you have available. Note that some applications require more than one space.

If you are looking for more room for a new application check this list for applications you don't use or that you seldom use and could move to a computer file in case you want it later. (Actually it is usually just as easy to go back to education.ti.com for the application if it is a genuine TI file.)

To remove an application:

1. Press

2. Choose 4:Delete...

3. Choose the type of item to be deleted. Applications are #8.

4. Press **ENTER** with the cursor on the application you want deleted.

5. You will be asked if you are sure. Choose 2:Yes (unless you've changed your mind!)

Now you have room for more!

Appendix C

Resetting the TI-73

Sometimes before taking a test your teacher may require that you reset your calculator.

To reset press [2ND] then [0] to get to MEMORY.

This screen should appear:

Choose 7:Reset…

You will usually want to choose 1:All RAM…

Choose 2:Reset

Note the message at the bottom. Any work on the homescreen, graphs, lists, etc. will be wiped clear. Applications will not be deleted. This gives you one last chance to change your mind.

If Applications also need to be removed see Appendix B for instructions.

Appendix D

Using the Variables Menu

When we perform certain operations, we assign values to variables or specific symbols. If we wish to use the assigned value in a later operation, we can find the variable or symbol in the Variables Menu.

Press [2ND] [APPS].   (Note that it says VARS above the Applications key.)

Of the choices you see there, you will most likely only need 2:Y-Vars and 3:Statistics. Let's check those out.

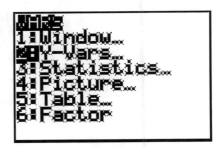

Choose 2:Y-Vars.

     If you have entered a complicated function in the Y= editor, you can use the function's name if you need to repeat it somewhere else. For example, if you want to graph the equation then you decide that you wish to use the equation in Solver, you can just enter Y1 in Solver.

Now go back to the VARS menu and choose 3:Statistics. Use the arrow keys to go over to EQ.

You will note that choice 1 says RegEQ. This stands for regression equation. **After** you have performed a regression, you can use this variable to enter the exact equation in Y1, on the home screen, or in Solver.

Choice 2 is the "a" that represents the slope in a linear regression and choice 3 is the "b" that represents the y-intercept in a linear regression. If they are in decimal form when you perform the regression, you can use these variables to convert your answers to fractions or mixed numbers.

Reference Sheet

Trigonometric Ratios	$\sin A = \dfrac{opposite}{hypotenuse}$
	$\cos A = \dfrac{adjacent}{hypotenuse}$
	$\tan A = \dfrac{opposite}{adjacent}$

Area	trapezoid $\quad A = \frac{1}{2}h(b_1 + b_2)$

Volume	cylinder $\quad V = \pi r^2 h$

Surface Area	rectangular prism $\quad SA = 2lw + 2hw + 2lh$
	cylinder $\quad SA = 2\pi r^2 + 2\pi rh$

Coordinate Geometry	$m = \dfrac{\Delta y}{\Delta x} = \dfrac{y_2 - y_1}{x_2 - x_1}$